London Bus
ONE BY ON
101–20ʊ

MATTHEW WHARMBY

TRANSPORT SYSTEMS SERIES, VOLUME 4

Front cover image: For many years the 101 linked London's docklands with their workforce living in the East End, but as the docks dwindled, so did the route. Historically, it was one of the major routes of Upton Park garage, but this closed in 2011 under Stagecoach and most recently Blue Triangle have taken over, with mid-career Volvo B9TLs like River Road-based **WVL 471** (LJ61 NXA), seen at Beckton bus station on 27 March 2021.

Back cover image: In the 2010s Alexander Dennis and Volvo developed hybrid models from their respective diesel predecessors and pitted the resulting E40H and B5LH against one another for the custom of London's bus operators. Go-Ahead took 311 Volvo B5LHs, 199 of them Wrightbus-bodied, and the WHV class, actually composed of two styles of Wrightbus Gemini body, is exemplified at Wimbledon on 12 June 2021 by Merton's **WHV 80** (BF65 WKE), new to Metrobus and still carrying its fleetnames but filling in on the 200 until the expected arrival of Optare MetroDecker EV electrics later in 2021.

Title page image: Electric buses look set to sweep London within the next decade and a half, although the level of British ownership in their manufacture has diminished. Chinese giant BYD's DD model has muscled its way to the forefront through an advantageous tie-up with Alexander Dennis, which bodies it with the Enviro400 City design. Here at Dagenham Heathway on 27 March 2021 is Stagecoach East London **14105** (LF70 YTZ), new into service at the beginning of the year and allocated to Rainham garage for the 174.

Opposite: One of the most important routes in central London, the 159 plies through Oxford Street and then heads south, crossing the river by Westminster Bridge (though, for most of its history, it has taken Lambeth Bridge). Having seen the gala last day of Routemaster buses in 2005, it spent the next two Arriva London South contracts operated by Volvo B7TLs and Wrightbus Gemini 2 Integrals, but in 2015 was tendered again and Abellio came out the winning bidder. Under Mayor Boris Johnson, the deployment of LT-class New Routemasters (better known as 'Borismasters') was different from the usual practice in that TfL owned the thousand-strong class and leased them to operators. Abellio thus received several dozen and put them into action from its Battersea garage, sharing this particular batch with LTs allocated earlier for the 3 and then, later ones still for the 68 and 211. This is **LT 614** (LTZ 1614), seen at Trafalgar Square on 13 September 2020.

Key Books
an imprint of Key Publishing Ltd.
PO Box 100
Stamford
Lincs PE19 1XQ

www.keypublishing.com

Copyright © Matthew Wharmby, 2021

ISBN 978 1 80282 031 7

Typeset by Matthew Wharmby

Introduction

Here is a snapshot in 2021 of London bus routes 101-200, with a photographic example or two of the type of bus operated on each route, in accordance with its Transport for London (TfL) contract applying at time of publication.

The modern London bus tendering system offers each route out for a period of five years; companies compete to run the routeing laid down in the tender and are awarded based on the most efficient bid, usually, but not necessarily, at the lowest price. Often, groups of routes are bid for under a combined price and, other than that, the models and internal specifications of buses (though not the livery, strictly all-red) are up to the operator. This has resulted in the continuing variety of interiors and fleetnumbering systems to be found on what, to the casual observer, appears to be a unified fleet in the manner of the old London Transport.

Four years into the five, the routes go out to tender again and, if companies have performed above an agreed level of punctuality, two more years are added, which has no bearing as such on who is awarded the next time. Routes can thus stay put with one firm for many years or decades, or bounce around, often coming back to an operator which might have lost before.

Matthew Wharmby
Walton-on-Thames
May 2021

In its wartime heyday the 101 fielded over sixty buses, transporting workers from their East End homes to the booming foundries of London's Docklands. With the decline of industry after that, ridership for the 101 fell away and, instead of 64 utility Guys as in 1951, Upton Park in 1993 could offer only twelve Titans. In the interim, RT operation lasted from 1954 to 1972, with two spells of Routemasters broken by a period (1978–79) with DMs. One-man operation (OMO) ensued in 1982 with Titans, and in 1994, just as London Buses Ltd was selling Upton Park's operating unit to Stagecoach, the pioneering low-floor single-deck Scanias (SLWs) entered service. They were gone by 2005, when the 101 was taken away from its historic North Woolwich terminus and bent off instead to Gallions Reach, the site of a new shopping mall that needed some foot traffic. Upton Park's closure in 2011 saw Barking take over, and this garage replaced the Tridents with new E40Ds when Stagecoach East London began a renewed contract in 2012. However, Blue Triangle made a successful bid the next time around and, in 2017, added it to River Road garage's extensive portfolio. Midlife Volvo B9TLs (WVLs), some of which had served with the East London Transit operation but which are now in all-red, are the staple.

LEFT: New to Merton in 2012 for the 249, WVL 477 (LJ61 NWL) spent its early career on the EL-group of East London Transit routes before Borismasters made it spare; on 17 April 2021 it is seen at East Ham on its normal route now, the 101.

BELOW: With a similar history as the bus above, River Road's WVL 469 (LJ12 CHC) is coming up to Beckton on 17 April 2021.

102

Brent Cross, North Cricklewood, Golders Green, East Finchley, Fortis Green Road, Muswell Hill, Bounds Green, Palmers Green, Silver Street, Edmonton Green.

ARRIVA LONDON NORTH (AD) – Volvo B5LH (HV)

Still longer than most London bus routes, the 102 has shifted subtly westward on its meandering route through north London. Palmers Green has had control for most of its life, at first with Enfield and Tottenham support and later adding help from Muswell Hill. The main allocation retained RT operation until 1978, though Muswell Hill's weekend participation had fielded RMs since 1963, then RMLs and finally DMs before coming off in 1982. OMO Ms replaced RMs in 1982 and continued for twenty years, though the route changed in 1988 through re-routing to Edmonton Green rather than Chingford, and again in 1992 when it was extended from Golders Green to Brent Cross. In 2002 it was converted from M to VLW and a contract retention in 2007 introduced Arriva London North's first Enviro400s (Ts), which completed two contracts of their own before HV-class Volvo B5LHs were acquired second-hand from Stagecoach in 2019.

RIGHT: Seen coming up to the 102's Edmonton Green terminus on 24 November 2019, HV 179 (BJ14 KSX) was formerly Stagecoach Selkent 13019, but its original owner returned it off lease after five years.

BELOW: On 27 March 2021 HV 186 (BG14 ONX), new as Stagecoach Selkent 13026, passes the 102's old Golders Green stand on its way to Brent Cross.

103

Rainham Station, South Hornchurch, Dagenham East, Becontree Heath, Oldchurch Road, Romford, Pettits Lane North, North Romford (Chase Cross).

ARRIVA LONDON NORTH (DX) – Wrightbus Gemini 2 (DW)

Linking Romford and Rainham via the eastern portions of Dagenham, the 103 was a early transfer into the newish North Street garage in 1953 and continued to operate from there for the next three and a half decades. RTs gave way to OMO SMSs in 1971 and DMSs followed in 1975, with Ts taking over in 1979. The solidification of the London border and the development of an entirely different public-transport ethos on the Essex side ensured that all forays of the 103 north of North Romford had ceased by the 1980s, and then came tendering to shake it all up again. In 1990 County Bus bid for the 103 and won it, putting in new Leyland Olympians, but a year later Grey-Green bought out the operation and repainted the buses it kept; it did so again when Arriva was instituted. After fifteen years, Stagecoach East London won the 103 in 2005 and North Street resumed control using new Dennis Tridents, and its retention in 2012 was accomplished with E40Ds. However, Arriva was not done yet and won the route back, now operating the 103 from Grays and amassing mid-life DWs for it.

LEFT: Twice a green bus garage (Eastern National until 1951 and London Country after 1970), Grays is now firmly integrated into Arriva London North and fields DWs on the 66, 103 and 370; here at Romford on 10 May 2019 is DW 202 (LJ09 SUO).

BELOW: On 17 September 2019 Grays' DW 234 (LJ59 AED), new to Clapton, is seen south of Romford station.

In trolleybus days a circular route emanating from Stratford picked around the busy areas immediately to the east and came back via West Ham. It was known in the Routemaster era as 272 and, when converted to flat-fare OMO, S1, but by 1989 it was decided to separate the circle into two and the 104 took the lower road. Upton Park Ts ran on Mondays to Saturdays and West Ham on Sundays, though the latter aspect was minibussed in 1992 and taken over by Stratford garage in the same year. By 1995, when Stagecoach East London was the owner and operator, the 104 was daily out of Upton Park with the latest Scanias, but in 2001 it was single-decked again with Dart SLFs to fulfil the low-floor imperative. Tridents restored the upper deck in 2003, but from 2011 ran from West Ham after Upton Park's closure. A contract renewal in 2012 specified new Enviro400s, and these ran until 2018 when the 104 was awarded to Blue Triangle. River Road thus amassed enough mid-life Enviro400s to use. In the longer term, plans exist to split the 104 again, with a new route 304 taking over half the current routeing.

RIGHT: E 276 (SN13 CJE), new to Northumberland Park on its own, has since transferred to River Road and on 17 April 2021 is seen heading south through East Ham.

BELOW: E 189 (SN61 BJJ), leaving Stratford on the new two-way alignment on 25 June 2020, is not 'FULL' at all, but social distancing regulations obliged the printing of such cards to deter passengers.

Historically anchored on Western Avenue, the 105 penetrated much further, as far as Hounslow to the west and Wandsworth Bridge to the east. By the outbreak of war it had settled down to link Shepherd's Bush and Southall, enjoying operation by the eponymous garages at those points. RT-family operation characterised three decades, Shepherd's Bush converting from RTL to RT in 1966 and neither here nor Hounslow upgrading to RM until 1978. In 1973 it was projected to Heathrow Airport, producing one of the longest routes on the London Transport system. Shepherd's Bush garage withdrew in 1981 and at the end of 1982 Southall phased in Metrobuses in crew mode, prior to OMO in 1983. When Southall closed in 1986, Hanwell took over, but the route was now too long for modern sensibilities, and in 1988 it was split into two overlapping sections, the eastern half at Alperton garage ultimately being given its own identity, 95, in 1992. Now terminating at Greenford Station, the 105 was reallocated to Alperton in 1993 and minibussed with MAs in 1995. Operation by London & Country in 1996 proved disastrous, and Centrewest took it over the next year, keeping the green Dart SLFs but from Alperton. It was then moved within First London to London Buslines and equipped with its own yellow Dart SLFs. Further reorganisation saw it double-decked in 2001 with TNs and put into Greenford garage, which kept it until 2011 when Metroline won; in came VW-class Volvo B7TLs from Perivale West. In 2018 London United won the contract and now operates Volvo B5LHs (VHs) from Hounslow Heath.

LEFT: On 24 April 2021 Hounslow Heath's VH 45268 (LF18 AXK) is seen at Southall Broadway.

BELOW: VH 45271 (LF18 AXA) passes through Greenford on 30 March 2021.

106

Finsbury Park Station, Lordship Park, Stoke Newington, Clapton, Hackney, Cambridge Heath, Bethnal Green, Mile End Gate, Whitechapel (Cavell Street).

LONDON GENERAL (NP) – BYD DD (Ee)

Once stretching clear across east London, the 106 was operated historically by various combinations of Athol Street, Leyton, Tottenham, Hackney and Poplar garages. Its original extent from Finsbury Park to Becontree began to contract westward after the 1960s, first pulling back to Poplar in 1971. In 1972 its RMs were replaced at Tottenham and Poplar, the two operating garages by then, with OMO DMSs but legendarily struggled, to the extent that RMs were restored in 1979. In 1981 the new Ash Grove garage took sole control and in 1982 put Titans in for a second and more successful attempt at OMO. The revitalisation of the Isle of Dogs saw an extension to Crossharbour in 1983. Over the decade, Ash Grove converted to Ms and back to Ts and in 1989 was compelled to pull the 106 back to Mile End Gate so that new local D6 could service the peninsula. Ash Grove's closure in 1991 saw Clapton Ms take over and in 1993 the southern terminus was established at Whitechapel. Single deck operation under Docklands Buses in 1996 was a step too far, and after Stagecoach East London acquired this company it replaced the Darts with Tridents. A retained contract in 2008 introduced Scanias and a move from Bow to West Ham, but in 2013 Arriva took over with DWs from Ash Grove (since reopened). In 2020 London General won the 106, putting into service new electric BYDs from Northumberland Park garage.

RIGHT: Multiple tendering victories for London General in 2020 prompted an order for forty-seven electric BYDs with Enviro400 City bodywork. Here at Bethnal Green on 2 May 2021 is Ee 36 (LF20 XMP) on the 106.

BELOW: Just south of Hackney Town Hall on 25 June 2020 is where we see Northumberland Park's Ee 1 (LF20 XLA).

107

New Barnet Station, Barnet Church, Arkley, Stirling Corner, Balmoral Drive, Borehamwood, Elstree, Canons Corner, Edgware Way, Edgware Station.

METROLINE (EW) –Alexander Dennis Enviro400 (TE) and Volvo B9TL (VW)

Route 107 unusually leaves the London border for Borehamwood and then pops back in on its core Edgware–Barnet link. In the process, it was London's longest bus route for two distinct spells, linking Queensbury and Enfield Lock, before the second separation of its eastern end in 1986 (as 307) took root. Switched from Enfield to Edgware garage at this point, the 107 was later passed to Atlas Bus on tender in 1989, but Metroline bought that company in 1994 and have kept hold of the 107 ever since, first with EDR-class Darts, then VPL-class Volvo B7TLs, then TE-class Enviro400s and today using the next diesel double-deckers available, VW-class Volvo B9TLs.

LEFT: Metroline have dual-sourced for so long that concentrating a single type of double-decker at any one garage has been impractical, despite the wastefulness of needing to source multiple sets of spares. The newest double-deckers along from the 107's previous 08-reg TEs were 11-reg VWs, despite Edgware not previously having been a VW operator, and on 20 July 2020 VW 1177 (LK11 EXM) is seen leaving its home.

108

Stratford International, Stratford City, Bow Church, Devons Road, Poplar, Blackwall Tunnel, North Greenwich, West Parkside, Blackheath, Lewisham.

LONDON CENTRAL (MG) – Mercedes-Benz Citaro (MEC)

The Blackwall Tunnel's only bus route, the 108 has always had the dilemma as to which way to head once south of that point, though to the north it has always been anchored on Stratford. It has served Crystal Palace, then Eltham and today Lewisham, with Morden Wharf the modern garage on behalf of London Central.

LEFT: When Red Arrow routes 507 and 521 were converted to electrics in 2016, fifty Citaros were made spare. Half of these left fleet strength but the rest were put into New Cross for the 108, later accompanying the route on its reallocation to Morden Wharf. Here at Lewisham on 17 April 2021 is MEC 20 (BD09 ZRA).

Taking over from tram routes 16 and 18 all the way down the Brighton Road to Croydon and Purley, the 109 was tremendously busy from the day of its introduction in 1951. Brixton and Thornton Heath garages shared responsibility with 88 RTs between them, but cars and TV cut into ridership and the PVR dwindled. By 1976, when RMs finally took over at each garage, 62 were needed, and in 1978 DMs appeared, though Brixton's allocation got Routemasters back in 1981 and Thornton Heath followed suit in 1982. In 1985 the Croydon–Purley leg was cut away to form new route 59, and, when OPO came in 1987, the Embankment loop was withdrawn in favour of a straightforward Trafalgar Square terminus. Thornton Heath DMSs were now in command, with Brixton Ms on Saturdays only. In 1990 Streatham replaced Thornton Heath and absorbed Brixton's allocation in 1991, only to close in 1992 and pass the 109 to a mix of Thornton Heath and Croydon, with Brixton at weekends and a return to Purley that lasted until 1998. Thornton Heath fielded Ts, then Ms and finally Ls, and had the route to itself again from 1994, though Brixton returned between 1996 and 1999. That year saw the 109 cut in half, losing everything north of Brixton. DLAs replaced the Ls in 2001 and Enviro400s (Ts) appeared in 2010, but in 2015 the 109 was awarded to Abellio and the capital's first MMC E40Hs appeared, operating out of Beddington Cross garage. These remain in service today.

RIGHT: Seen in the revamped Croydon town centre that forms the 109's modern southern terminus is 2503 (YY64 TZC) on 30 August 2019.

BELOW: Heading south through Streatham on 31 May 2020 is Beddington Cross's 2498 (YY64 TYW).

110

Hounslow, Hanworth Road, Powder Mill Lane, Whitton, St. Margaret's, Richmond, Kew Gardens, Gunnersbury, Turnham Green, Hammersmith (Bus Station).

LONDON UNITED (AV) – Alexander Dennis E20D (DLE)

New in 1936, the 110 was a local route linking Twickenham and Hanworth, with an extension later added to Cranford. Its unique run through some backstreets that it had to itself kept it alive, though rarely with more than a dozen buses from Hounslow garage; RTs gave way to MBSs in 1969 and SMSs took over between 1971 and 1976 when LSs were introduced. In 1978 the 110 was reallocated to Fulwell, which double-decked the route again in 1979 with new Metrobuses. Tendering took the route away from LBL in 1987 and London Country South West stepped up, with ex-Manchester Leyland Atlanteans, but contracts were shorter then and Westlink replaced them in 1990, using Optare Delta-bodied DAF SB220s. The Hounslow–Cranford section dwindled and came off in 1995, when conversion to Dart took place. In 1998 Hounslow had the 110 back and in 2002 briefly used Optare Excels before a new London United contract in 2003 specified its own DPS-class Dart SLFs. It bounced thereafter between Fulwell (2011) and Hounslow again (2014), and in 2017 new DLEs (E20Ds) furnished another retained contract. The most significant event in the 110's history came in 2020, when it was diverted over part of the H22 to Richmond and then swallowed up the 391 in its entirety to Hammersmith!

LEFT: The 110 is now on the long side and the service to Hammersmith risks getting snarled up by Twickenham rugby days. On 12 December 2020 Hounslow's DLE 30333 (YX68 UVU) is in King Street, having previously been part of the stock for the 391.

BELOW: On 5 April 2021 DLE 30058 (SN17 MVG) is seen coming through Richmond.

111

Kingston, Hampton Court, Hampton Station, Hanworth, Hounslow, Heston, Cranford, Harlington Corner, Heathrow Airport Central.

LONDON UNITED (AV) – Scania N230UD (SP)

At first a local route linking Hounslow and Hanworth, the 111 enjoyed an improbable Saturday extension all the way to Hammersmith, though this was pulled back during the 1950s; at the other end an extension to London Airport was mounted in 1955, though this was quickly reduced to peak hours and pulled back to Cranford in 1960. In 1964 the 111 made its first attempt to reach Kingston, again on Saturdays only, but then OMO came in 1969 Hounslow's six RTs were replaced by four MBSs. The transfer of these elsewhere in 1971 brought SMSs instead, plus the revival of its drive towards Kingston, at first as far as Hampton. LSs appeared in 1976 and the Kingston extension was applied throughout in 1978. In 1981 the Heathrow leg also returned on a daily basis and stuck. Double-deckers returned in 1982 in the form of Ms and these continued until 2000 when route-branded VAs (Volvo B7TLs) were introduced; similar VPs also featured until a new contract with what was by then the incumbent London United added Scanias in 2010. These are contracted to last until 2022 at least and, if Hounslow performs to TfL's satisfaction, for two years after that.

RIGHT: Setting off from Kingston via a recently-constructed bus-only exit road to the west is Hounslow's SP 40182 (YT10 XCF) on 8 August 2020.

BELOW: Coming into Kingston on the lowered road under the railway bridge on 10 September 2020 is SP 40202 (YR10 FGK).

112

Ealing Broadway, Hanger Lane, Stonebridge Park, Neasden, Brent Cross Shopping Centre, Finchley, North Circular Road, North Finchley.

METROLINE (W) – Alexander Dennis E20D (DEL)

The 112 has historically battled the North Circular Road's notorious traffic before being reduced twice. At its full length it ran from Palmers Green to Ealing Broadway and then, on Sundays, on to Hampton Court; in charge was Palmers Green garage, with help at various points from Hendon, Willesden, Cricklewood and Alperton into the RT era, with Stonebridge settling in as the southern garage from 1962. In 1970 it was cut in half, the eastern end beyond Finchley with the Palmers Green allocation becoming new route 212, and this set the 112 up for its SMS conversion in 1971. DMSs came in 1976 and in 1978 the 112 was restored to its Palmers Green terminus. Stonebridge closed in 1981 and up stepped Cricklewood with Ms, though in 1988 Pan Atlas took over with Leyland Lynxes. An extension in 1990 took the route south from Palmers Green to Wood Green. R&I Buses were the next operator from 1994, using new MAN 11.190s; the 112 was cut back to Brent Cross, with the eastern half becoming 232 this time. R&I was taken over by MTL London in 1995; MTL London in turn passed to Metroline in 1998 and Cricklewood resumed control in 2000 (at first with Ms and then DPL-class Darts). Perivale garage had it in 2003, but in 2004 TGM took over. This company became Travel London in 2006 and Abellio in 2009, but in 2014 Metroline won it back and Cricklewood introduced DE-class Enviro200s. In 2020 new MMC E20Ds (DELs) took over, serving a re-routing via Madeley Road on its last leg to Ealing Broadway. An extension to North Finchley was implemented at the same time.

LEFT: Intended for use elsewhere, the 112's DELs took a long time to enter service, but on 24 April 2021 at North Finchley DEL 2605 (YX19 OVJ) is well bedded in.

BELOW: Setting off in the other direction from Ealing Broadway in order to serve Madeley Road is Cricklewood's DEL 2597 (YX19 OVA) on 24 April 2021.

<table>
<tr><td>

113

</td><td>

Oxford Circus, Baker Street, St. John's Wood, Swiss Cottage, Hendon Way, Brent Cross, Hendon Central, Apex Corner, Edgware Station.

METROLINE (EW) – Volvo B5LH (VMH)

</td></tr>
</table>

Beginning on the Watford Way dual-carriageway as a local service, the 113 gradually expanded, first outwards towards Edgware and then, in 1939, taking its classic form into town to Oxford Circus. It was Hendon garage's major route for many years, operating RTs (1952), RMs (1962), RMLs (1976) and Ms (1986), but closure in 1987 saw its reallocation to Edgware, where it has stayed. Edgware's varying levels of association with Cricklewood after that meant that the latter enjoyed responsibility from 1993 to 1999, by which time both bases were part of Metroline. In 2001 new VPL-class Volvo B7TLs (VPLs) took over and TEs replaced those by the end of the decade, at which point (2009) the 113 was re-routed out of Oxford Street to stand at Marble Arch. This was reversed in 2017, by which time the complement was TEH-class E40H hybrids, but in 2018 a new contract saw the introduction of Volvo B5LHs (VMHs).

RIGHT: On 21 March 2021 Edgware's VMH 2441 (LK18 AFX) is in Baker Street heading south towards Oxford Circus.

BELOW: At the Edgware end of the 113 on 20 July 2020 is VMH 2437 (LK18 AFN).

114

Mill Hill Broadway Station, Watling Avenue, Burnt Oak, Queensbury, Kenton, Harrow, Porlock Avenue, South Harrow, Victoria Road, Ruislip Station.

METROLINE WEST (UX) – Volvo B5LH (VWH)

Little of the 114's original configuration survives other than the basic South Harrow–Harrow leg. A year after its introduction in 1934, the route was extended west to Rayners Lane and thence to its familiar Ruislip terminus in 1966. Harrow Weald garage maintained control; when the 114 was withdrawn between Harrow Weald and Edgware in 1970, the long-serving RTs gave way to SMSs and the garage wrung a decade out of the otherwise unhappy Swifts before LSs took over in 1980. It was in 1983 that the route's defining change took place, with the swapping of the 140's long leg to Mill Hill, and in this form it became busy, though single-deckers didn't leave until 1987 when a mix of Ms and Vs took over under the Harrow Buses operation. Tendering proved unkind and the 114 was one route lost in 1991, passing to BTS with new orange Leyland Olympians. This outfit lasted a quarter-century here, rebranding to Sovereign in 1996 and acquiring DAF DB250RS(LF) low-floor double-deckers in 2001 before replacing them with Volvo B7TLs (VLEs). 2016 saw the contract won by Metroline West, who had to base it at Uxbridge garage, some distance away from Ruislip, with new Volvo B5LHs.

LEFT: Uxbridge's VWH 2357 (LK67 CXP) is in Station Road, Harrow, on 20 July 2020.

BELOW: Making the right turn from Station Road towards Harrow Bus station on 2 September 2018 is VWH 2173 (LK16 DFN). This Volvo B5LH was an earlier example put into Uxbridge for the 222.

Today's route of this number is the 15B renumbered, which in itself was the second try at sectionalising the extremely long and busy trunk route 15 at its eastern end so as to permit OPO and thus make some savings. It began with Dennis Tridents (TAs) from Upton Park, but that garage's closure in 2011 saw operation moved to West Ham. In 2017 the 115 was awarded on tender to Blue Triangle, which bought new E40Hs for River Road garage to operate it. At some point shortly it will need to move out of this garage to a new base.

RIGHT: On 28 February 2021 River Road's EH 153 (YW17 JVG) is coming up to Canning Town bus station, the mid-point of the 115.

BELOW: On its first day in service, 27 August 2017, EH 141 (YW17 JUK) is seen at Aldgate East, a couple of stops along from the 115's City start point.

17

116

Hounslow (Bus Station), Hounslow Heath, North Feltham, Bedfont Green, Ashford Hospital.

LONDON UNITED (HH) – Volvo B5LH (VH)

Historically a dead-straight run south-west from Hounslow, the 116 has lost its western end to Staines but regained double-deckers. Trolleybus replacement saw it extended to Hammersmith in 1962 but this fell back in 1971, when SMSs replaced Hounslow's RTs. LSs followed in 1976 and continued when Westlink was established in 1986. TGM took over in 1991 but passed this operation to London & Country in 1992, and in 1996 Hounslow returned under a London United contract, first with Lynxes, then briefly Ms and Ls and, in 2001, Dart SLFs. Hounslow Heath garage (formerly of Westlink) resumed operation in 2006 and kept it until 2020, when the 116 passed to Hounslow; however, Hounslow Heath took it back in 2021.

LEFT: Full-time double-deck operation returned to the 116 in 2015 with the delivery of new VH-class Volvo B5LHs. These moved with the route to Hounslow in 2020 but came back to Hounslow Heath on 12 June 2021. On that day, VH 45147 (LJ15 LBA) is seen leaving Hounslow bus station.

117

West Middlesex Hospital, Isleworth, Hounslow, Hounslow Heath, Feltham, Lower Feltham, Ashford, Woodthorpe Road, Staines.

METROLINE (AH) – Alexander Dennis Enviro200 (DE)

Back in its Staines–Hounslow form again after working onward to Shepherd's Bush between 1962 and 1979, the 117 in LT days was run by Hounslow garage, followed by Westlink (1986), TGM (1991), London & Country (1992), Armchair (1996), Metroline (2004), Abellio (2006) and Metroline again (2016), with single-deckers ranging from LSs to Darts, Dart SLFs and Enviro200s. In 2021 it will pass to London United with Mercedes-Benz Citaro Ks.

LEFT: Two spells of Brentford operation have characterised the 117's last quarter-century, first as Armchair and then, on that company's subsequent acquisition by Metroline, under that identity. Here in Hounslow town centre on 3 June 2017 is Enviro200 DE 996 (LK09 ENH).

The 118 has meandered round the less obvious thoroughfares of Mitcham and Streatham Vale since 1936, though, as with almost all London bus routes, its ends have changed. From the outset the responsibility of Streatham garage, which shared it on and off with Merton, the route linked Clapham Common and Raynes Park until 1969, when the western end was curtailed at Morden. Merton's contribution had come off by then, but in 1972 Brixton joined in, first on Sundays and then daily; from 1978 Brixton had the route to itself. Despite the 118's suburban nature, one-manning wasn't made feasible until 1985, when Ms took over. Streatham took back the 118 in 1987 and converted it to L operation, at which point it was re-routed away from Streatham Hill so that the 137 could pass Brixton garage. This made the Clapham Common end less popular and in 1990 the 118 was re-routed to Brixton station. Having lost its Ls for Ms, Streatham closed in 1992 and Brixton returned, now with Ts but in 1993 replacing them with Ms. On Sundays by now it was Dart-operated and this part moved to Norwood. Evening DR operation soon followed, but daily double-deck operation was the case again from 1997. In 2001 tendering awarded the 118 to London General, bringing back Merton. PVLs lasted until 2011 when Es took over, and these have stayed, though some shuffling has been evident in recent years, with Metrobus Croydon taking over in 2017 and then being supplanted almost immediately by Stockwell.

RIGHT: The 118's batch of 60-reg Es has wandered from garage to garage in their eleven years so far, though always staying tethered to the same route. Now based at Stockwell, E 142 (SN60 BZP) is at Morden on 13 November 2019.

BELOW: On 7 July 2019 E 147 (SN60 BZV), now in all-red like the rest of its batch, works through Mitcham.

119

Purley Way (Colonnades), South Croydon, East Croydon, Shirley, West Wickham, Hayes Station, Hayes Lane, Bromley South, Bromley North Station.

METROBUS (C) – Volvo B5LH (WHV)

Linking Croydon and Bromley since 1939, the 119 has been altered repeatedly at the western end and amidships, with multiple suffixed variations operating at weekends. The basic route was one of Bromley garage's stalwarts and used RTs between 1951 and 1976, followed by RMs until 1984. Titans arrived late that year in crew mode and lost their conductors in 1985, at which point the Saturday 119B was removed and the 119 became daily. Between 1961 and 1992 its western terminus had been Thornton Heath High Street, but this was pulled back to West Croydon and in 1996 pushed off in the other direction to Croydon Airport in a swap for the routeing of the 194. In 1998 the 119 was awarded to Metrobus and has stayed there ever since, though Croydon garage replaced Orpington in 2007 and the original Volvo Olympians gave way to Scanias and then Volvo B5LHs (WHVs).

LEFT: Croydon's B5LH WHV 64 (BF65 WJK) is at East Croydon's vestigial set of eastbound bus stands on 3 November 2019.

BELOW: Central Croydon has been revamped in recent years, with the resultant change to stand arrangements. The 119 is one to pass through this new layout, and on 31 August 2019 WHV 63 (BF65 WJC) is doing so.

Always covering Heston Road and Norwood Green on its way north from Hounslow, the 120 was less certain over the years as to where to proceed from there; at first it was west to Hayes & Harlington Station and from 1960 it was pulled back to Southall. In 1965 it was projected northeastward from this point to terminate at Greenford. Southall garage's RTs on the route lasted all the way to 1978, when DMS OMO was instituted, and at the end of 1989 Southall upgraded to Ms. In 1986 Southall closed and Hounslow took over, and a year later the southern end was amended this time, with a short extension from Hounslow Heath to Beavers Farm Etate over the former 257. In 1988 the 120 was withdrawn between Southall and Greenford and in 1990 the Beavers Farm extension was removed. In preparation for conversion to Dennis Lance SLF (LLW) low-floor operation, the 120 was extended from Southall in a third direction, this time to Northolt over the 232. The LLWs were introduced in 1994 and lasted until 2000 when VAs (Volvo B7TLs) restored the upper deck; the operator since 1994 had been London United. In 2009 Scanias (SPs) took over and in 2012 another London United contract introduced E40Hs (ADEs). Since 2017 Metroline has been in charge, using Volvo B5LHs (VWHs) from Perivale West garage.

RIGHT: On 24 April 2021 Perivale West's VWH 2282 (LK17 CZJ) heads south at Southall Broadway.

BELOW: At the Hounslow end of the 120 on 5 April 2021 is seen VWH 2270 (LK17 CZT).

121

Turnpike Lane Station, Wood Green, Palmers Green, Southgate, Oakwood, Enfield Town, Ponders End, Enfield Lock, Enfield Island Village.

ARRIVA LONDON NORTH (E) – Wrightbus Gemini 2 (DW)

From tiny acorns; for many years this route eked out a twilight existence as the lone carrier from Enfield across the Lea Valley Reservoir to Chingford, exchanging its three Enfield-based RTs for four RFs in 1966, but in 1980 it was transformed into a busy suburban route through its extension to Oakwood and then on via the 298A to Turnpike Lane. Palmers Green took over with DMSs and in 1982 upgraded to Ms, though that year saw Enfield given back an allocation that ultimately became the only one. Enfield Lock now became the terminus. In 1992 Palmers Green was restored and had the route to itself for ten years. The long-lived Ms were finally replaced by DLAs in 2002, but the eternal exchange with Enfield began again at this point, this garage gaining back a share and then the entire route, with two Ms added at schooldays by Leaside Travel, Arriva London North's private-hire arm. Enfield has maintained control, with DWs replacing the DLAs in 2013 and continuing for the next Arriva London North contract starting in 2018. Since 2000 the eastern end has worked to Enfield Island Village.

LEFT: New in 2013, Enfield's DW 561 (LJ13 CEO) is taking the roundabout leading to Southgate station on 11 March 2020.

BELOW: On 25 February 2018 DW 576 (LJ13 CJO) is passing Wood Green Underground station.

122

Crystal Palace, Sydenham, Forest Hill, Brockley Rise, Ladywell, Lewisham, Lee Green, Eltham Green, Westhorne Avenue, Academy Road, Woolwich, Plumstead Garage.

STAGECOACH SELKENT (PD) – Alexander Dennis E40H

When it had the entirety of the 186 appended to its Woolwich–Bexleyheath run in 1964 and simultaneously received an extension east to Slade Green, the 122 became the longest bus route in London, but for all its length it was reliable and could reach its new Forest Hill terminus in an hour and three-quarters. The original Plumstead garage had responsibility, with RTs until 1978 (when the Bexleyheath–Slade Green leg came off), RMs until 1980 and then crew MDs. In 1981 the new Plumstead garage took over, replacing the MDs with Titans in 1983 and then converting the 122 to OMO, but in 1984 the route's excessive length was addressed by separating the Woolwich–Bexleyheath end and giving it to Bexleyheath garage to run. Both garages received Ls in 1986, but in 1988 the eastern end was removed to become Bexleybus route 422 and the 122 now terminated at Woolwich. Stability has ensued, with Plumstead still in control across privatisation by Stagecoach Selkent in 1994, and just the vehicle complement has changed; from Ls (with T support again between 1990 and 1995 plus straying Volvo Olympians) to Dennis Tridents in 1999 and finally, from 2014, whatever's not in the front line, spanning Scanias to Enviro400s to the newest Volvo B5LHs and E40Hs.

RIGHT: One of the E40H MMCs new to Plumstead for the 53 in 2016, 12391 (YX16 OHG) is at Lewisham on 18 April 2019.

BELOW: An earlier 'classic' E40H out of Plumstead is 12274 (SN14 TXO), new for the 54 in 2014 but now part of the mix commonly to be seen on the 122; on 6 February 2021 it is in Woolwich town centre.

123

Ilford, Gants Hill, Walthamstow, Tottenham Hale, Tottenham, Bruce Grove, Westbury Avenue, Turnpike Lane Station, Wood Green Station.

ARRIVA LONDON NORTH (AR) – Wrightbus Gemini 2 (DW) and Volvo B5LH (HV)

Long but quick about it, the 123 replaced trolleybus route 623 in 1960, sharing RMs from Tottenham and Walthamstow garages. Until 1968 its western terminus was Manor House, but it was re-routed after that to Enfield Town and added a Wood Green allocation in lieu of Tottenham. Palmers Green pitched in shortly after, but came off with Wood Green when the 123 was one-manned with DMSs in 1977, losing its Winchmore Hill–Enfield section in the process. In 1983 Walthamstow was upgraded to Titans and in 1988 the route was withdrawn between Wood Green and Winchmore Hill, fixing it in place ever since. The London Forest debacle of 1991 took it off this LBL subsidiary and awarded it to Capital Citybus, which put it into Dagenham with new yellow Leyland Olympians; two retentions later TNLs (Tridents) took over in 2001, but the winners in 2005 were Arriva London North, whose Tottenham garage came back and now used new Volvo B7TLs (VLAs). This company has also enjoyed two tender renewals, upgrading the 123 to DW in 2014 and, from that point until 2016, operating it from Edmonton. With the influx of HVs into Tottenham, plenty can be sure to turn out on today's 123 alongside its incumbent DWs.

LEFT: On 20 February 2021 Tottenham's DW 463 (LJ61 CEF) is at Turnpike Lane, serving a bus station much expanded and improved at the start of the century.

BELOW: The Ilford end of the 123 on 18 April 2019 sees DW 470 (LJ61 CDF) coming in after a long but speedy journey along mostly wide roads.

124

Eltham (Southend Crescent), Middle Park, Mottingham, Dunkery Road, Grove Park, Downham, North Downham Estate, Sangley Road, Catford (St. Dunstan's College).

STAGECOACH SELKENT (TL) – Alexander Dennis E20D

Linking Catford and Eltham ever since replacing double-deck route 209 in 1937, the 124 has only ever been operated by Catford garage. Its traditional Forest Hill terminus at the west was not abandoned until 1987, and beyond Eltham it has variously reached Woolwich, Welling and/or Bexley Hospital, the latter usually on a Sundays (when that arm wasn't separate as 124A). RMs replaced its RTs in 1971 and were then supplanted in 1972 by OMO DMSs, with Titans taking over Catford in 1983. Minibus operation has been the 124's lot since 1990, owing to a re-routing into narrow Kingsground; at first these were MW- and SR-class Mercedes-Benz 811Ds. A further re-routing into even narrower backstreets near Grove Park in 1993 meant that only the shortest minibuses could be specified; in 1999, after privatisation to Stagecoach Selkent, these were DRL-class Darts. 8.9m SLD-class Dart SLFs followed in 2001 and the contract applying from 2012 introduced E20Ds of the same length.

RIGHT: On 17 April 2021 Catford's 36531 (LX12 DHL) is in Eltham High Street. Blinds with fluorescent yellow characters have held out here for longer than on most buses.

BELOW: 36528 (LX12 DHG) is coming up to the Catford Bridge end of a typical route 124 journey when sighted on 23 August 2020.

The 125 has linked North Finchley and Southgate since 1937, with extensions at both ends; in 1951 it was projected south to Golders Green and to the east it served Highlands Hospital, with a Sunday run on to Winchmore Hill becoming daily in 1971. SMS OMO was instituted at this point, from Finchley garage, and DMSs took over in 1977 with Ms in turn in 1980, but in 1978 the 125 was withdrawn south of North Finchley. A peak-hour extension to Hendon was restored in 1979, lasting until 1982. A Sunday extension to Enfield Town was added in 1986 and continued after Grey-Green took over in 1987, with Fleetlines and then Metrobuses. Changes in 1991 and 1992 first saw an extension south to Finchley Central and then the withdrawal of the Sunday leg to Enfield Town. As Grey-Green evolved into Arriva London North-East it upgraded to Volvo Citybuses and then, in 1998, was reallocated within the group to Palmers Green. In 2002 it was transferred again to Edmonton and regained Ms, but in 2003 new DLPs took over, with the garage changed again, to Enfield. Back at Palmers Green from 2006, it began another Arriva contract but towards the end of this moved to Edmonton again, in 2014. Under Metroline from 2015, the 125 used Volvo B5LHs (VWHs) from Potters Bar and still does after renewal in 2020. New ground was broken in 2019 with an extension from Finchley Central to Colindale.

LEFT: On 3 November 2020 Potters Bar's VWH 2042 (LK64 EHL) heads out of Southgate Station. The 125 is also host to numerous VMHs wandering from the 317.

BELOW: Pointing the other way at Southgate on 24 April 2021 is VWH 2059 (LK64 EJE).

126

Eltham (Southend Crescent), Mottingham, Dunkery Road, Grove Park, Bromley South.

METROBUS (MB) – Alexander Dennis E20D

Always anchored on the Eltham–Bromley North corridor, the 126 took its current number in 1940 and has seen extensions at either end, the longest being westward to Beckenham Junction. One of Bromley garage's portfolio of routes, it operated RTs up to 1968 when OMO came with MBs; DMSs restored the upper deck to the route in 1974, but shortages compelled it to be taken away again in 1979 with the advent of LSs. Other than a brief period between 1985 and 1987, when Titans furnished an extension north of Eltham to Woolwich, it has been single-deck ever since. The Woolwich leg came off in 1989 and the following year minibuses came, with a mix of MRLs and DTs. The latter soon transferred away and Mercedes-Benz 811Ds (MAs) were added a little later. In 1994 the 126 passed on tender to Kentish Bus with new Darts, falling back from Beckenham Junction to Bromley South at the same time and, due to being operated from Dartford garage rather than the troubled Lewisham, was kept hold of. In 2001 another contract introduced Dart SLFs, by which time Kentish Bus was known as Arriva Kent Thameside, and these were repainted from blue to red in order to stay in place. In 2013 Metrobus won, using E20Ds, and a renewed contract here has seen these buses continue after a refurbishment.

RIGHT: A number of the original route 284 E20Ds moved over to London Central when Metrobus lost that route, but the rest held in place on the 126. Here at the current, not particularly satisfactory, Bromley terminus on 28 February 2021 is 755 (YX13 AHC).

BELOW: On 17 April 2021 733 (YX11 CTK) is in Kentish Way, Bromley.

127

Tooting Broadway, Southcroft Road, Mitcham, Mitcham Junction, Hackbridge, Carshalton, Wallington, Woodcote Green, Purley Station.

METROBUS (C) – Alexander Dennis E40D (E) and Volvo B9TL (WVL)

New in 1981, the 127 turned over the southernmost bit of the 77 to OMO and used DMSs from Merton until conversion to LS a year later. However, it came into its own in 1984 with an extension south from Wallington to Purley over the old 234, at which point DMSs returned but now operated by Croydon garage. In 1986 it was won by London Country, using Leyland Atlanteans from Chelsham and, as this company evolved into London & Country, new Volvo Citybuses took over. By the time it had fallen under the control of this company's own Croydon premises, internal reorganisation in 1995 produced the Londonlinks brand and, at the tail end of this operation in 1997, Volvo B6 single-deckers took over. Staff shortages compelled its surrender, however, and in 1998 London General Ms took over, with subcontracts to Blue Triangle (Ms) and Stagecoach Selkent (DALs). A permanent contract was awarded to Mitcham Belle in 1999 using new Dart SLFs, but this company was unable to hack it in the long term; its successor incarnation from 2004, Centra, was even worse and Metrobus took over in 2005, beginning with hired PVLs (Volvo B7TLs) from London General and then its own Scanias. That's where it's stayed, though with a considerable vehicle variety that persists today.

LEFT: Once Metrobus came under Go-Ahead responsibility, it began to receive standard vehicles on transfer and these replaced the 127's Scanias; here at Mitcham on 7 July 2019 is E40D E 217 (SN61 DDV).

BELOW: Smartly repainted, Croydon's E 219 (SN61 DDY) heads south from Tooting Broadway on 31 May 2020.

128
Claybury Broadway, Barkingside, Gants Hill, Ilford, Green Lane, Becontree Heath, Roneo Corner, Queen's Hospital, Romford Market, Romford Station.

STAGECOACH EAST LONDON (NS) – Alexander Dennis E40D

Introduced in 1993 to replace the 129's eastern section, the 128 fielded Ts from North Street but in 1997 was won by Harris Bus and treated to blue and green Volvo Olympians. Harris Bus became East Thames Buses in 2000 and red repaints ensued, followed in 2002 by the 128's conversion to Volvo B7TL operation. In 2004 it was extended from Ilford to Claybury Broadway to replace the rest of the 129 and in 2005 was won by Arriva with VLAs from Barking. Fourteen years later North Street came back under a new Stagecoach contract and this time uses transferred 12-reg E40Ds.

RIGHT: New to Bromley garage for the 208 in 2012, 10150 (LX12 DHA) was made surplus in 2019 by the loss of that route to Metrobus and transferred to North Street to take over the 128 from Arriva London North. On 13 September 2019 it is coming up to the Romford station terminus.

129
Greenwich (Cutty Sark), East Greenwich, West Parkside, North Greenwich Station.

LONDON CENTRAL (MG) – Volvo B9TL (WVL)

New in 2006 as a local link from Greenwich to North Greenwich via the shops of East Greenwich, the 129 began with Dart SLFs from Travel London's Walworth. Go-Ahead won it in 2011 and put on EDs from New Cross; double-deckers (Es and WVLs) came in 2012 for the Olympics and stayed. Since 2017 Morden Wharf has run it.

RIGHT: On 17 April 2021 New Cross's Volvo B9TL WVL 354 (LX60 DWD) still in its almost vanished original livery, is seen at the Greenwich, Cutty Sark terminus of the 129. Plans to push the route on beyond Greenwich to Peckham came to naught, but more recently there exists a consultation as to whether it might not be better served replacing the 180 to Lewisham.

130

Thornton Heath (Clock Tower), Norwood Junction, Woodside, Shirley Hills Road, Addington Village, Fieldway, Headley Drive, New Addington (Vulcan Way).

ABELLIO (BC) – Alexander Dennis E20D

Always the Croydon–New Addington link, the 130 can count itself lucky that Croydon Tramlink was not so popular as to wipe it out of existence. This in fact was the actual plan before it was realised that, even when demoted to Darts, the 130 was still used by passengers. In order to dissuade them from taking the bus instead of the trams, however, TfL re-routed it away from Croydon to Norwood Junction in 2003 and its subsequent extension to Thornton Heath has actually brought it back to one of its old termini, although by a different route. Historically Croydon garage's responsibility, the 130 was operated in the 1960s with the last of the RML delivery run and sprouted not only 130A, 130B and 130C variants, but five express routes numbered C1-C5, which later became express adjuncts to the 130 and 130B themselves and finally just X30, which came off altogether upon the advent of Tramlink. DM operation of the 130 ensued in 1975 and DMS OMO in 1982, with Croydon adding Ts in 1991 and then replacing those in 1992 with Ms; by 2000 it was predominantly L operated. In 2002 it was converted to LDR operation and in 2003 won by Metrobus, with Dart SLFs. After two contracts with them, the 130 was won by Abellio and uses E20Ds from its Beddington Cross garage north of Croydon.

LEFT: On 27 August 2017, the second day of the 130's tenure with Abellio, E20D 8191 (SN17 MWV) is at Norwood Junction, on the way to its new (or old) terminus at Thornton Heath.

BELOW: Beddington Cross's 8192 (SN17 MWW) is at New Addington, Salcot Crescent, as rain breaks out on 2 May 2021.

131

Kingston, New Malden, Raynes Park, Worple Road, Wimbledon, South Wimbledon, Merton, Colliers Wood, Tooting Broadway.

LONDON GENERAL (AL) – Volvo B9TL (WVN)

The slower of today's two options between Kingston and Wimbledon, the 131 was historically oriented to the west and only became associated with Wimbledon when it replaced trolleybus route 604 to that point in 1962. Merton garage joined Norbiton and both operated RMs, sharing in changing proportions throughout the DMS era (1973) and beyond. An extension at the other end covered the entire 155 on Sundays for many years, taking the 131 all the way to the Embankment, but in 1971 its western extremity was curtailed at West Molesey. Norbiton gained Metrobuses in 1979, but Merton retained DMSs and was reduced to a Sunday allocation only from 1980. In 1987 the route was put out to tender and won by London Country South West, which started it off with ex-Manchester Leyland Atlanteans before that company's evolution into London & Country two years later introduced new Volvo Citybuses. Westlink won the 131 in 1990 and operated with Titans from Kingston; this firm's takeover by London United in 1995 brought it to Fulwell and in 1996 upgraded it to Volvo Olympians, which were replaced in 2001 by Dennis Tridents. In the 2010s Scanias (SPs) and Volvo B7TLs (VLEs) were the staple, but in 2017 London General won the 131 and use a mix of WVNs and WHVs, once more from Merton.

RIGHT: Go-Ahead's takeover of much of First London's assets in 2013 included a large number of Volvo B9TLs available, which were renumbered WVNs. Here at Kingston on 21 March 2021 is Merton's WVN 38 (BV10 WVL), new as First VN 37841.

BELOW: WVN 44 (BV10 WWP), ex-First VN 37857, is at Tooting Broadway on 31 May 2020. The 131 was extended here in 2007.

132

North Greenwich Station, West Parkside, Kidbrooke, Eltham, Avery Hill, Blackfen, Blendon, Bridgen, Bexley, Bexleyheath (Shopping Centre).

LONDON CENTRAL (BX) – Alexander Dennis Enviro400 (E)

In its long existence, the 132 has roved all over the map, but has always been anchored on its Blackfen and Blendon core. It has variously terminated at Dartford, Lewisham and Woolwich and has been a circular route twice. Sidcup and Bexleyheath garages were in charge in the RT era, the latter from 1964, but in 1970 OMO came with new SMs. DMSs restored the upper deck in 1974 but shortages obliged a second spell with SMs later in the decade. Bexleyheath took Ts to replace its DMSs in 1983, by which time the 132 was a circular again. Bexleyheath's closure in 1986 restored the route to Sidcup but, with its tendering and award to Boro'Line Maidstone in 1988 it resumed a basic Eltham–Bexleyheath configuration that remains today. Kentish Bus took over Boro'Line in 1992, keeping hold of the mix of Leyland Olympians and Volvo Citybuses; another operator change in 1998 introduced Harris Bus, with blue and green Optare Excels. This company stumbled hard and in 2000 its new owner transformed it into East Thames Buses, with red repaints. Double-deck Volvo B7TL operation predominated, but had given way to DAF SB120s by the time Go-Ahead bought East Thames Buses in 2008 and folded it into London General. In 2009 the 132 was extended from Eltham to North Greenwich, additionally being reallocated from Belvedere to Bexleyheath. Double-decking with Es followed in 2014.

LEFT: Bexleyheath garage tends to chuck anything at the 132, from Es, ENs, WVLs and even, on 17 April 2021 at Eltham station, WVN 48 (BL61 ADU), new to First as VN 37946 and acquired in 2013.

BELOW: Properly belonging to the 89, E 245 (YX61 DPZ) has been turned out on the 132 on 2 May 2021 and is seen at North Greenwich.

133

Liverpool Street Station, Bank, Monument, London Bridge, Borough, Elephant & Castle, Kennington, Brixton, Streatham Hill, Streatham Station.

ARRIVA LONDON SOUTH (BN) – Alexander Dennis E40H (HA) and Volvo B5LH (HV)

Hard worked on its traditional routeing from the City to South Croydon, the 133 shared RTs from Brixton and Croydon into the 1960s, though retrenchment began in 1964 with its withdrawal back to Thornton Heath. Between 1958 and 1968 the entirety of both routes 43 and 143 were appended on Sundays, bringing it all the way to Hendon Central on that day, but after that ceased, a second major cutback rendered the southern terminus Streatham Garage from 1971. RTs were replaced by DMs in 1975, though RMs took over in 1981. Crew DMSs returned in 1984 and upon OPO in 1985, the DMSs were joined by Ms from the 95, which was withdrawn so that the 133 could be extended to Tooting Broadway. Any combination of DMSs and Ms, plus three Hs, endured until 1990 when the 133 was tendered and LBL's London General subsidiary took it, with new Volvo Citybuses (VCs) from Stockwell. These lasted twelve years, spanning privatisation in 1994, until the return of Ms in 2002, followed by Volvo Olympians (NVs), and then, to go with a new London General contract in 2003, new Volvo B7TLs (WVLs). Mandela Way garage was in charge between 2007 and 2010, after which Arriva won the 133 with new Ts (Enviro400s) from Norwood. For 2017's retained contract, reallocation to Brixton was accompanied by the delivery f new E40Hs (HAs) and refurbished Volvo B5LHs (HVs),

RIGHT: Leaving the new Streatham stand carved out for the 60, 133, 159 and P13 is Brixton's HV 136 (LT63 UJS) on 31 May 2020.

BELOW: E40H HA 41 (LK66 HBJ) is at the Elephant & Castle on 12 September 2019.

134

Warren Street, Mornington Crescent, Camden Town, Kentish Town, Tufnell Park, Archway, Highgate Station, Muswell Hill Broadway, Friern Barnet, North Finchley.

METROLINE (PB) – Optare Metrodecker EV (OME)

Very long and very busy, the 134 had its wings clipped by the coming of the Victoria Line in 1968, but continued to link far north London with Tottenham Court Road. It kept Potters Bar garage in business, with help from the original Holloway and later Muswell Hill. Routemasters were established by 1965, but in 1973 doored crew operation was phased in, first with DMSs and then purpose-built DMs. RMs returned in 1982, but in 1983 the 134's withdrawal north of Barnet Church saw Potters Bar's allocation removed. Muswell Hill then replaced the RMs with Ms in 1986 and took off their conductors. In 1988 a surfeit of spare Titans was put into Muswell Hill, which continued until the garage's closure in 1990, though in 1989 the 134 was pulled back further south still, to Friern Barnet. When Finchley garage took over from Muswell Hill (with a mix of Ts and Ms) the route was extended west to North Finchley, but Finchley closed in 1993 and Holloway took over. New Tridents (TPs) replaced Ms in 1999, and in the next decade low-floor VPLs, TPLs and TEs could all be seen. In 2017 the 134 was reallocated back to Potters Bar and in 2019 converted to electric Optare Metrodeckers (OMEs), though the withdrawal of the Warren Street–Tottenham Court Road section in 2019 was an unnecessary irritant.

LEFT: A little dumpy with its short rear overhang, the Optare Metrodecker has nonetheless managed to keep its kerb weight below twelve tons. On 1 April 2019 Potters Bar's OME 2656 (YJ19 HVG) is at Archway.

BELOW: On 24 April 2021 OME 2678 (YJ69 DFY) is leaving North Finchley on a journey going only as far towards town as Mornington Crescent.

135

Old Street Station, Shoreditch, Liverpool Street Station, Aldgate, Limehouse, Canary Wharf, Heron Quay, Spindrift Avenue, Island Gardens, Crossharbour (Asda).

DOCKLANDS BUSES (SI) – Volvo B5LH (EHV)

The current incarnation of route 135 was introduced in 2008 to link Old Street with the Isle of Dogs peninsula and, at that point, was contracted to Arriva, who used Enviro400s (Ts) from Barking. After one full contract term, with two years added for good performance, the route was tendered again and this time won by Go-Ahead, which allocated it to Docklands Buses at Silvertown, using a batch of the rare Enviro400-bodied Volvo B5LH. In 2016 its Docklands end was re-routed to approach Crossharbour from the opposite direction after having served Spindrift Avenue in lieu of the D3.

RIGHT: Seen at Aldgate East on 27 August 2017 is Silvertown's EHV 4 (BL15 HBK).

BELOW: Coming past the relocated Island Gardens DLR station on 25 June 2020 is EHV 6 (BL15 HBJ).

136

Elephant & Castle, Rodney Road, North Peckham, Southampton Way, Peckham, New Cross, Lewisham, Catford, Downham Way, Grove Park Station.

STAGECOACH SELKENT (TL) – Alexander Dennis E40D

Introduced in 1994 as a straight renumbering of the 36B, the 136 was less significant than its predecessor had been, but at least restored double-deck operation. These were Titans and later Olympians, based at Catford (the ownership of which passed from London Buses Ltd to Stagecoach six months after the route's creation). In 1999 low-floor operation came with Dennis Tridents and after two contracts, Enviro400s took over in 2012. In 2014 a useful extension from Peckham to the Elephant & Castle was added to take pressure off the 343, but this brought the route into the area specified for the ULEZ low-emissions zone. That obliged the route to be upgraded to new buses, which could only be achieved by taking the E40D MMCs meant for the 179 in 2018.

LEFT: Seen in Lewisham High Street on the afternoon of 17 September 2018 is Catford's 11002 (YY18 TLF).

BELOW: Having followed the 343 road through North Peckham, 11059 (YX68 UMZ) is arriving at the Elephant & Castle on 11 April 2019.

137

Marble Arch, Hyde Park Corner, Knightsbridge, Sloane Square, Chelsea Bridge, Queenstown Road, Clapham Common, Kings Avenue, Streatham Hill (Telford Avenue).

ARRIVA LONDON SOUTH (BN/N) – Wrightbus New Routemaster (LT)

The quintessential jack-of-all-trades where London bus routes are concerned, the 137 linked large parts of both north and south London with the centre and, in so doing, united a myriad of different social circumstances. Inevitably, contraction had to come in the face of traffic; in 1987 it lost its Oxford Circus–Archway section and four years later its Streatham Hill–Crystal Palace leg was separated. It is still substantial enough for all of that, and retained crew operation until 2004, latterly from Brixton garage. In the postwar era it had seen a combination of Victoria and Norwood, with participation on and off from Camberwell, Clapham and Streatham. OPO was instituted with DWs, which lasted a decade until Borismasters took over in 2014. In 2017 Norwood regained an allocation and since then, the share with Brixton has fluctuated so that since 2020 they have been in near parity. One unhelpful change executed in 2017 withdrew the 137 between Marble Arch and Oxford Circus.

RIGHT: The 137 has actually had two separate batches of Borismasters, the original contingent having since moved elsewhere within Arriva. New to Norwood in 2017 was LT 962 (LTZ 2162), which is seen on 21 March 2021 at the awkward Marble Arch stand.

BELOW: Also a Norwood motor, LT 977 (LTZ 2177) is crossing Marble Arch on 25 June 2020.

Always the link between Bromley North and Coney Hall south of Hayes, the 138 has enjoyed two separate existences under that number and both of them have at one time been projected north of Bromley. The current incarnation made its return in 1990, taking back its core from the former B1, and with its Bromley garage SRs, got as far north as Catford via outer sections of Downham transferred from the L3, another withdrawn minibus route. In 1994 the 138 was taken over on tender by Kentish Bus but this operation proved too much to handle and the route found itself passed from garage to garage within the overall owning group, working from Londonlinks Croydon, Bromley and back at Lewisham all in 1995 before defeat was admitted and the route surrendered. Metrobus proved a better option, inheriting the 138's Metroriders and in fact staying in control ever since. The progression of bus types has thus gone from Darts to Dart SLFs, Enviro200s and now E20Ds. In 2004 the Bromley North–Catford section was turned over to route 336 and the original format resumed.

LEFT: Metrobus has amassed a sizable number of 8.8m E20Ds in various batches and even fleetnumber sequences, but now mixes them all up. Coming into Bromley High Street on 30 August 2019 is Orpington's 163 (YX61 ENC).

BELOW: On 2 May 2021 155 (YX60 FUV) is in Bromley High Street.

139

Waterloo Station, Trafalgar Square, Piccadilly Circus, Oxford Circus, Baker Street, Lisson Grove, Abbey Road, West Hampstead, Golders Green Station.

METROLINE (W) – Volvo B5LH (VWH)

New in 1992, the 139's task was to localise the 159's northwestern section up to West Hampstead and, probably more importantly, to keep Chalk Farm garage in business when its routes were otherwise falling away to tender. Its closure happened nonetheless, in 1993, and Holloway took over its RMs, though used Ms on the evening and Sunday OPO duties where Chalk Farm had fielded Ts. In 1998 it was converted to OPO with new Dennis Dart SLFs (DMLs) allocated to North Acton, and these moved with the route to Cricklewood in 2000. New double-deckers came with the 2003 Metroline contract, plus an extension from Trafalgar Square to Waterloo, and in 2011 hybrids came in the form of Alexander Dennis E40Hs (TEHs). In 2017 it passed to Sovereign, which used Volvo B5LHs (VHs and VHRs) from Edgware, but in 2020 came back to Metroline, for which Cricklewood now employs Volvo B5LHs (VWHs).

RIGHT: New to Perivale West for the 7, VWH 2023 (LK14 FCA) was displaced by newer examples of the VWH class and made available for the 139 at Cricklewood; it is seen crossing Piccadilly Circus on 15 September 2020.

BELOW: The 139's Waterloo–Oxford Circus link has proven invaluable and indeed is now unique; VWH 2016 (LK14 FBN) is almost across Waterloo Bridge on 27 March 2021.

140

Hayes (Asda), Hayes & Harlington Station, Yeading, Northolt, South Harrow, Porlock Avenue, Harrow, Wealdstone, Harrow Weald Garage.

METROLINE (HD) – Volvo B5LH (WHV)

The 140 has historically ploughed one of the longest furrows in the capital, between Harrow and Heathrow, but the length is able to be worked efficiently and it is only since 2019 that the southern end has been snapped off. In fact, until 1983 it went on from Harrow all the way to Mill Hill and even after that a renaissance in 1985 took it to Edgware, running the same distance at a higher latitude. The route has been Harrow Weald garage's raison d'être and was notable for not receiving RMs to replace its RTs until 1978. M OMO ensued in 1983 and in 1987 it fell under the Harrow Buses scheme, with a mix of leased Mark 2 Metrobuses and second-hand Volvo Ailsas, all in red and cream. After that came to an end in 1990 Ms resumed control and after the privatisation of Metroline in 1994 gained blue skirts. Since then the 140 has been at the forefront for vehicle replacement, with TAs coming in 1999, TPLs in 2002, VPs in 2004 and VWHs in 2016; some of the last were branded for a local exercise anchored on Hayes and Harlington. In 2019 it was withdrawn between the station of that name and Heathrow, though an express X140 introduced at the same time maintains the link and at a much faster clip.

LEFT: Fussy in its application and obscuring the view out, the branding carried on Harrow Weald's VWH 2188 (LK16 DGZ) proved no better than the earlier Barkingside-area variant. It is seen in Harrow on 2 September 2018.

BELOW: Coming up to Harrow and points beyond along Station Road on 20 July 2020 is VWH 2205 (LK66 DWX).

141

Palmers Green, Wood Green, Turnpike Lane, Manor House, Newington Green, Hoxton, Old Street, Moorgate, Bank, Monument, London Bridge Station.

ARRIVA LONDON NORTH (AD) – Volvo B5H (HV)

New in 1961 to replace trolleybus route 641 between Winchmore Hill and Moorgate, the 141 later had the old 179 appended to it in its entirety, resulting in a lengthy cross-London route going all the way to Grove Park in the south-east. As time went on, Wood Green and New Cross thus operated broadly independent sections coincidentally both numbered 141, and crew operation remained until 1985 (though DMs had been used between 1977 and 1981). Upon OPO conversion, New Cross used Ts and Wood Green Ms, with Catford coming in to help the southern section and the two halves operating as one on Saturdays. In 1992 this format was severed, with the southern end broken off as 172 and the 141 turned over to Grey-Green on tender, with bizarre double-deck rebuilds of Volvo B10M coaches. Once Grey-Green's owner had acquired Leaside Buses from London Buses Ltd and both became Arriva companies, it was considered expedient to put the 141 back into Wood Green in 1998 and Metrobuses returned, lasting until 2001 when VLWs replaced them. In the interim, the route had been projected to its London Bridge terminus of today. 2006 saw it pushed north from Wood Green to Palmers Green and gained a Palmers Green garage allocation, with the latter taking over in full in 2015. Hybrid Volvo B5LHs (HVs) are now the staple fare.

RIGHT: On a sunny 25 February 2018 Palmers Green's HV 72 (LJ62 BVE) is passing Wood Green Underground station.

BELOW: Bank junction is where HV 60 (LJ62 BYU) is when captured on 18 April 2019.

142

Watford Junction, Bushey, Stanmore, Canons Corner, Edgware, Burnt Oak, Colindale, West Hendon, Staples Corner, Brent Cross Shopping Centre.

SOVEREIGN (BT) – Alexander Dennis E40H (ADE)

Always the carrier of passengers out of London to the north-west, the 142 has crossed the border at Bushey Heath and continued on to Watford Junction for a century, for much of that time giving work to Edgware garage. In fact, only two structural changes have been made, the first being its withdrawal between Edgware and Kilburn in 1970 (when SMS OMO was instituted), and the second being an extension from Edgware to Brent Cross in 1976. The 142's SMSs managed to last a decade but were replaced by Ms in 1980, and in 1986 tendering saw London Country bag it, with Leyland Olympians (LRs) from Garston. And, under a variety of names, that was where it stayed for thirty more years' worth of retained contracts. Over the years the identities on bus sides progressed from London Country North West via Watford Bus to Arriva serving Watford, while the colour scheme changed from two shades of green to green and grey, then blue and yellow, then aquamarine and stone and finally red. The generations of buses operated comprised new Leyland Olympians (1990) and DAFs (2003), but eventually Garston became a liability to Arriva and its tenders dropped away. In 2018 Sovereign won and put transferred E40Ds into action from its Edgware premises (coincidentally, half of the LT site).

LEFT: Coming out of the approach road to Edgware bus station and the pair of garages beyond it on 8 June 2018 is ADE 40416 (YX12 FNY), new to London United at Hounslow but refurbished for the 142.

BELOW: A hundred yards or so further on from the left turn taken by the bus above is Edgware's ADE 40403 (YX12 FNJ) on 20 July 2020.

143

Archway Station, Highgate Village, East Finchley, East End Road, Finchley Central, Hendon, Hendon Central, Brent Cross Shopping Centre.

METROLINE (W) – Alexander Dennis Enviro200 (DE)

Abandoning its cross-London pretensions during the war for a straightforward Archway–Hendon Central configuration, the 143 has continued along that basic core ever since, though it's never been busy, with single-deckers deemed sufficient today and OMO as early as 1968. The MBs instituted then gave way to DMSs in 1975 and, in 1976, the opening of Brent Cross furnished a new terminus. In 1978 Hendon garage replaced Holloway. Ms were introduced in 1980 and continued when Hendon closed in 1987 and operation passed back to Holloway, but later that year it was reallocated to Edgware. In 1991 it was converted to minibus with SRs, which alone could manage a re-routing into backstreets round Finchley Central. Cricklewood assumed responsibility in 1994, by which time Darts (DRs) were in use, but one schoolday journey endured, operated first by Edgware with an M and then by London Traveller (later Metropolitan Omnibus). Cricklewood fell under Metroline and was privatised with it in 1994; Dart SLFs new in 1998 (DLDs) had blue skirts. Holloway ran the 143 again between 2000 and 2002, but in 2005 Perivale West replaced Cricklewood. New DEs came with 2010's contract and in 2012 were transferred to Cricklewood, which continues to run them today.

RIGHT: Setting off from Brent Cross on 11 September 2016 is Cricklewood's DE 1128 (LK10 BYU).

BELOW: Almost at the Archway end of a typical route 143 journey on 21 April 2019 is DE 1138 (LK10 BZE).

144

Edmonton Green Station, Silver Street, Wood Green, Turnpike Lane, Hornsey, Priory Road, Alexandra Park, Muswell Hill Broadway.

ARRIVA LONDON NORTH (WN) – Wrightbus Gemini 2 (DW)

Although the number 144 is associated with the Great Cambridge Road, the original pair of routes became the 217 and 231 and this particular incarnation is actually the renumbering of the 144A, created to dip off the main drag and serve Wood Green. With the previous 144's renumbering to 444 in 1991 the number had become free and it was re-used in 1994 to accompany the entry into service at Wood Green of new low-floor Scania single-deckers (SLWs). These were joined in 1998 by three DAF SB220s (DLPs), but in 1999 double-deck operation was restored with a batch of new DLAs. After their lifespan had played out, the 144's next generation of buses comprised DWs, which in the most recent years have found themselves bolstered by sizeable numbers of the HV class of hybrid Volvo B5LHs wandering from the 29.

LEFT: Edmonton Green's signature three tower blocks have been joined in recent years by a couple more, one of which is on the left in the background of Wood Green's DW 481 (LJ61 CCK), seen on 11 March 2020.

BELOW: On 20 February 2021 DW 478 (LJ61 CCD) pauses in Wood Green.

145

Leytonstone, Green Man, Wanstead, Redbridge, The Drive, Ilford, South Park Drive, Longbridge Road, Becontree, Dagenham Village, Dagenham (Asda).

STAGECOACH EAST LONDON (BK) – Alexander Dennis Enviro400

With an Ilford–Dagenham link at its core, the 145 has fluctuated at either end, taking passengers all the way to Chingford and, at the other end, to busy workplaces at the Ford foundries in Dagenham. It has mostly been the responsibility of Barking garage, with Seven Kings assistance on and off and even participation from Upton Park and Forest Gate. Its RT era ended in 1974 with conversion to DMS OMO and the Ilford–Chingford end mostly turned over to the 179, but in 1980 Titans came to Barking and were still there to return in 1991 after the 145 spent five years as an Ensignbus contract with blue and silver former DMSs. Upon Ensignbus's takeover the route had taken over the 147's roads to Redbridge and in 1993 was pushed onward to Leytonstone. That year saw conversion to Darts (DWs) but these buses were too small for the passenger traffic and, when Stagecoach acquired both East London and Selkent in 1994, redeployed full-size Dennis Lances (LAs) to the 145. A year later these left for Ribble and Optare Deltas (DAs) replaced them. Long Dart SLFs characterised the 2001 contract, but double-deckers returned in 2003 as Tridents. Since then two generations of Enviro400 (one batch in 2011 and MMC E40Ds in 2016) have been in charge.

RIGHT: New in 2016, Alexander Dennis E40D 10326 (SN16 OKH) of Stagecoach East London's Barking garage serves Ilford's one-way system and its accompanying cinema complex on 24 November 2019.

BELOW: Going in the other direction on 5 June 2016 is 10327 (SN16 OKJ) at Ilford station.

Passing through some charming countryside to the immediate south of its modern Bromley North terminus, the 146 kept its RTs all the way to 1978 simply because nothing since built could handle the narrow roads it served. However, Bristol LHs (BLs) put into Bromley garage instituted OMO at that point. In 1985 the route was put out to tender and up stepped local independent Crystals, with a variety of van-like minibuses and eventually two StarRiders. Crystals lasted just the one term, the 1991 tender being won by Metrobus, a growing local that kept hold of the 146 for the next quarter-century. The shortest available Darts in blue and yellow gave way over the years to the shortest Dart SLFs in all-over red, but in 2016 the streak was broken and Stagecoach won the 146; Bromley could now resume control, with an E20D.

LEFT: A small batch of E20D MMCs was taken in 2016 for Bromley to resume control of the 146 and 336; seen at Bromley South on 30 August 2016 is 36611 (YX16 OJZ).

BELOW: Going only as far as Keston when espied entering the fiddly bus-only lane in central Bromley on 17 April 2021 is Bromley's 36617 (YX16 OKV).

147

Ilford High Road, Browning Road, East Ham, Upton Park, Prince Regent Lane, Custom House, Keir Hardie Estate, Canning Town (Bus Station).

BLUE TRIANGLE (RR) – Alexander Dennis E40D (E)

It wasn't until 1954 that the 147 gained its signature section through some narrow streets on the fringes of East Ham and its consequent long association with Upton Park garage. RT operation gave way to SMS OMO in 1971, followed by DMSs in 1975 and Ts in 1982, by which time it was linking Redbridge and East Ham. In 1986 the Ilford–Redbridge section came off and shortly after that its southern section was re-routed to Kier Hardie Estate and eventually Canning Town. Barking garage took over in 1993 but Upton Park came back in 1999, now using Scanias until Tridents appeared in 2001. Not long before Upton Park closed, West Ham inherited the 147 in 2010, but in 2016 it was awarded to Blue Triangle, which uses refurbished E40Ds (Es) from River Road.

RIGHT: New to Mandela Way for the 453 and then spending 2014–16 at Camberwell, E40D E 169 (SN61 BGY) was refurbished for the 147 and on 13 September 2020 is seen at Ilford.

148

Camberwell Green, Elephant & Castle, Westminster Bridge, Victoria, Hyde Park Corner, Marble Arch, Lancaster Gate, Notting Hill Gate, Shepherd's Bush, White City.

LONDON UNITED (S) – Wrightbus New Routemaster (LT)

New in 2003 as part of the expansion pack funded by the Congestion Charge, the 148 avoids the built-up areas and as such has become tremendously busy. Always the responsibility of London United's Shepherd's Bush garage, it has progressed from Volvo B7TLs (VAs) to Scanias (SPs) and finally Borismasters (LTs).

RIGHT: Shepherd's Bush-based LT 129 (LTZ 1129) is coming through Victoria on 24 September 2019. In May 2021 it was announced as renewed by London United for another five years with its existing Borismasters.

149

London Bridge Station, Liverpool Street, Shoreditch, Dalston, Stoke Newington, Stamford Hill, Seven Sisters, Tottenham, Edmonton Green Station.

ARRIVA LONDON NORTH (AR) – Wrightbus New Routemaster (LT)

Arrow-straight up and down the Hertford Road, the 149 replaced trolleybus route 649 that had been doing the same thing until 1961. Both ends have since been retracted; the north has come back from Waltham Cross to Ponders End and, since 2004, Edmonton Green, whilst its run beyond Liverpool Street via Southwark Bridge to Waterloo and Victoria dwindled and finally disappeared in the 1990s. Instead, changes associated with the Jubilee Line Extension in 1999 saw the 149 pushed south to its current terminus at London Bridge. RMs inaugurated the route and were still there until OPO in 1987, though between 1974 and 1980 it had seen it allocated DMs and, from 1980–84, the plush ex-Green Line coach Routemasters (RCLs). Edmonton and Stamford Hill garages shared it, but in 1986 Edmonton closed and Enfield took its share; occasionally a place was found for a Tottenham allocation, both before and after the closure of Stamford Hill in 1995. Ms were the staple of OPO and lasted until 2001 when new DLAs took over, but in 2004 articulated Mercedes-Benz Citaro Gs (MAs) were introduced, based at Edmonton. Lea Valley garage took over in 2005 but gave it up to Tottenham when double-deckers (DWs) returned in 2010. Since 2015 it has been operated by Borismasters (LTs).

LEFT: Tottenham's LT 600 (LTZ 1600) reposes at the rebuilt London Bridge bus station on 1 November 2018. The removal of the roof has put an end to the fierce crosswinds that used to blow through here.

BELOW: Edmonton Green, where LT 587 (LTZ 1587) is seen on 11 March 2020, has been the 149's northern terminus since 2004, with a vestigial 349 taking passengers onward.

150

Becontree Heath, Green Lane, Ilford, Gants Hill, Barkingside, Fullwell Cross, Hainault, Manford Way, Chigwell Row.

ARRIVA LONDON NORTH (DX) – Alexander Dennis Enviro400 (T)

Long taking buses out through the top of the London border into Essex, the 150 was actually withdrawn in 1986 and subsumed into the 247 as a bifurcation, but this didn't work and the 150 was reconstituted in 1988 in its Chigwell Row–Ilford form, with Seven Kings Titans as before, plus North Street on Sundays and later daily. In 1992 Optare Deltas (DAs) were allocated to the route, but when Seven Kings closed in 1993 these went with it to Barking. In 1997 the 150 was one of three routes awarded to Harris Bus, which took it on with blue and green Volvo Olympians based at Thurrock, but this company faltered and soon became unable to cope. It was sold in 2000 and became East Thames Buses, with operation from Ash Grove, as far from line of route to the west as Thurrock had been to the east. In 2002 new Volvo B7TLs (VWLs) brought low-floor operation and in 2004 the 150 was extended to Becontree Heath over the withdrawn 129. In 2005 First won it and put on its own Volvo B7TLs (VNWs). Next time around, in 2010, Arriva were the winners and allocated new Enviro400s (Ts) from Barking. These have stayed around for the next successive contract and, for a spell from 2017, carried blue accents as part of a branding exercise covering routes operating through Barkingside.

RIGHT: Wearing the discreet but unsuccessful Barkingside branding, Barking's T 175 (LJ60 ATZ) makes the protected left turn at Ilford station on 18 April 2019.

BELOW: At Gants Hill on 15 September 2020, T 179 (LJ60 AUF) is southbound towards Ilford.

151

Wallington (Shotfield), Hackbridge, Green Wrythe Lane, St. Helier Hospital, Sutton, Cheam, North Cheam, Worcester Park Station.

LONDON GENERAL (A) – Volvo B9TL (WVL)

New in 1984, the 151 linked Wallington and Worcester Park and it still does, though has served different termini in the interim. It began with DMSs from Sutton, and these were still in place in 1988 when the western end was diverted at North Cheam to Lower Morden. However, in 1991 this section was devolved to the 413 as a minibus and the original terminus restored. A second attempt was made to cut it back upon conversion to LDP-class Dart SLF in 1996 this time as far as Cheam, but complaints about the lost link forced its restoration again in 1997. Sutton, in the person of London General, have also kept hold of the route, double-decking it in 2006 with refurbished PVLs. TfL still hadn't learned their lesson about removing the link to Worcester Park and in 2008 withdrew the 151 west of North Cheam, only to put it back in 2011, and there it has stayed. DOEs were included in the upgrade accompanying contract renewal in 2011, and these share the route with various transferred examples of WVLs and Es, plus WHVs wandering from the 93.

LEFT: Late in the day on 24 April 2021, Sutton's DOE 7 (LX58 CWV) is crossing North Cheam.

BELOW: On 5 April 2018 WVL 364 (LX60 DWP) is in the Sutton one-way system heading south. This bus was new to Bexleyheath but came later to Sutton.

152

Pollards Hill, Eastfields, Mitcham, Colliers Wood, Merton, South Wimbledon, Wimbledon Chase, Raynes Park, New Malden (Fountain).

LONDON GENERAL (AL) – Alexander Dennis Enviro200 (SOE)

Always skirting Wimbledon proper to the south on its way from Mitcham, the 152 has ever since enjoyed the dilemma of what to do when beyond the most obvious next catchment points to the west, and indeed it's served most of them in one form or another; Kingston, Esher and Hampton Court or Chessington. The responsibility of Merton by the 1960s, the route exchanged its RTs for MBs in 1970 and DMSs appeared in 1974. From 1980 decline set in; the 152's diversion at Tolworth to Surbiton in that year saw several roads leading to Hampton abandoned to buses altogether and in 1982 it was demoted to LS operation. In 1987 it was withdrawn between New Malden and Surbiton and pointed instead to Kingston, and in the following year regained DMSs upon its transfer to Sutton garage. However, the reallocation of Sutton's excess to a new site at Colliers Wood in 1990 included the 152, and Merton absorbed Colliers Wood a year later, bringing it back. In 1991 it was converted to MRL minibus and withdrawn west of New Malden, but east of Mitcham it was projected over withdrawn minibus route 352 to Pollards Hill. In 1996 new LDP-class Dart SLFs took over but in 2001 Mitcham Belle won the route and put on its own Dart SLFs. Mitcham Belle's tenure was unhappy and the company was purchased by Centra in 2004, but the even worse performance after that obliged surrender in 2006 and Travel London stepped in with Enviro200s. In 2016 back came Merton under London General.

RIGHT: Merton use a mix of SEs and SOEs on the 152, this capture of 5 April 2021 at the New Malden terminus being E20D SE 147 (YX61 BXP), transferred from Docklands Buses.

BELOW: Optare Esteem-bodied SOE 4 (LX09 AYJ) passes through Mitcham's thankfully de-pedestrianised town centre on 7 July 2019.

153

Finsbury Park, Holloway, Barnsbury, Copenhagen Street, Islington, St John Street, Barbican, Moorgate (Finsbury Square).

LONDON GENERAL (NP) – BYD D8UR (SEe)

Restoring the service to Barnsbury, lost when the 172 was pulled back to King's Cross in 1982, the 153 on its 1984 introduction linked Archway and the Angel using Holloway Ms, being extended within its first year to Tottenham Court Road. The extension was taken away in 1987, however, when London Country North West took over with green Iveco minibuses, and not returned when that company was obliged to turn the route over to London Buses Ltd a year later. Red Ivecos now appeared and in turn were replaced by new StarRiders in 1989, but in 1992 its award to Capital Citybus brought change at both ends. The 153 now linked Finsbury Park and Smithfield and used yellow Mercedes-Benz 811Ds from Northumberland Park (or, between 1998 and 2000, Hackney). Another change in 2001, accompanied by an extension to Liverpool Street, awarded it to Hackney Community Transport (or CT Plus), whose first and second contracts used Caetano-bodied Dart SLFs (HDCs) and its third, awarded in 2013, E20Ds (DAs). In 2018 London General, inheritors of Capital Citybus's Northumberland Park garage, won the 153 and have introduced new electric BYD/ADL single-deckers.

LEFT: Setting off from Finsbury Park on 16 August 2019 is SEe 67 (LJ67 DKO).

BELOW: A little further on from the above picture, Northumberland Park's SEe 66 (LJ67 DKN) has passed under the railway bridge on 25 February 2018 and will shortly peel off to the south.

154

West Croydon (Bus Station), Duppas Hill, Waddon Station, Roundshaw, Wallington, Carshalton Beeches, Benhill Avenue, Sutton, St. Helier Station, Morden Station.

LONDON GENERAL (A) – Alexander Dennis Enviro400 (DOE)

Probably the quieter of the two Morden–Croydon links, the 154 has abandoned its ambitions beyond the latter point, leaving them to the 157. It was new in 1959 as a straight replacement for trolleybus route 654 and kept its Carshalton garage in operation for five more years, after which Sutton took over, operating with assistance now and again from Thornton Heath and Croydon. RTs operated until 1973 when DMSs took over, and these lasted until 1992 when Metrobuses completed their filtering into Sutton. The only major changes structurally have been the diversion past Carshalton Beeches station in 1977, the withdrawal between West Croydon and Crystal Palace in 1981 and the diversion to serve Roundshaw in the same year. After the privatisation of London General, Sutton garage's holding company, in 1994, the 154 was converted to NV-class Volvo Olympian (NV) operation in 1997, to EVL-class Volvo B7TLs in 2002 and to Optare-bodied Enviro400s (DOEs) in 2009. These last have lost their original dark grey skirted livery for all-over red on refurbishment.

RIGHT: On 2 September 2018 Sutton's DOE 47 (LX09 AXW) is setting off from Morden.

BELOW: DOE 17 (LX58 CXG) is in central Croydon on 30 August 2019, about to serve Fairfield Halls on its way to Morden.

155

Tooting (St. George's Hospital), Tooting Broadway, Tooting Bec, Balham, Clapham South, Clapham Common, Stockwell, Oval, Kennington, Elephant & Castle.

LONDON GENERAL (SW) – Volvo B5LH (WHV)

The direct replacement for tram routes 2 and 4 since 1951, the 155 found it hard to defeat the brutal traffic found on the Clapham Road and in the modern era has had to be curtailed at either end. In the crew-operated era it picked round the Embankment in a loop, and a couple of seasons even saw a Sunday extension over the entirety of the 131 all the way to Hersham! This all fell away and in 1977 Merton's RTs gave way to RMs, though crew operation didn't end here until 1986, by which time crew DMSs had been in place for a couple of years. Now the convolution could start; off came the Embankment loop in 1984 in favour of a run to Aldwych and that too was pulled back to Elephant & Castle in 1987. In 1990 the 155 was split as 155 and 355 and the main service re-routed to Vauxhall, and not long after Ms had replaced the DMSs in 1991, the crazy decision was made to single-deck both 155 and 355 with 8.5m Darts (DWs and DRs). The Vauxhall diversion was cut back to Stockwell at this point and when double-deckers (Ts and then Ms) returned in 1996 the 155 was restored to the Elephant. Single-deckers came back in 1999 as LDP-class Dart SLFs, when the route was also diverted at Tooting to St George's Hospital so that the 219 could inherit the last leg on to Wimbledon. The next contract, in 2004, put the upper deck back using new PVLs (Volvo B7TLs). Stockwell and Merton juggled allocations thereafter but, after new WHVs took over in 2015, Stockwell was given full control in 2017.

LEFT: The Wrightbus Gemini 3-bodied Volvo B5LHs new to Merton for the 155 have since transferred to Stockwell; on 12 September 2019 WHV 83 (BD65 EVM) is at the Elephant.

BELOW: At the current southern end of the 155, WHV 85 (BD65 EVP) has come off the main road at Tooting on 30 July 2020, approaching the hospital.

156
Wimbledon, Alexandra Road, Southfields, Wandsworth, Clapham Junction, Queenstown Road, Battersea Park, Nine Elms, Vauxhall Station.

ABELLIO (QB) – Alexander Dennis Enviro400

New in 1983 as a means of localising the southernmost end of the old 77A and then inheriting the old M1's leg to Morden, the 156 began with Merton DMSs. In 1985 it was pushed beyond Clapham Junction to Vauxhall in the peaks but in 1987 lost its roads between Raynes Park and Morden to new route 163; at this point Stockwell took over operation. Just as conversion from DMS to M was beginning in 1991, it was rationalised to Clapham Junction–Morden and converted to DR-class Darts from Merton again. The DRs were subsequently reallocated and MRL-class Metroriders became the staple as privatised London General supplanted London Buses as the operating company. In 1997 tendering awarded the 156 to Limebourne with a quantity of new Dart SLFs, but this company came to pieces at the end of 1998 and emergency operation by a host of firms was implemented until the heirs to Limebourne could pull themselves back together and restock the 156 shortly after with new Caetano bodied Dart SLFs. Connex bought the new Limebourne in 2001 and have kept hold of the 156 ever since, through renamings to Travel London and today's Abellio. Dennis Tridents restored the upper deck in 2002, when the Vauxhall leg was restored, and were replaced in turn by Enviro400s.

RIGHT: The 156 now serves Vauxhall again, but takes a different approach to that point than the first time around. Battersea's Enviro400 9503 (LJ09 OLU) is on stand on 26 May 2018.

BELOW: With a better-masked blind box than in the previous shot and new blinds to go in it, 9503 (LJ09 OLU) is at Clapham Junction on 2 February 2020.

157

Crystal Palace, Anerley, Norwood Junction, Selhurst, West Croydon, Waddon, Stafford Road, Wallington, Carshalton, Wrythe Lane, St. Helier, Morden Station.

ARRIVA LONDON SOUTH (TH) – Alexander Dennis Enviro400 (T)

The busier option of two routes linking Morden and Croydon, the 157 continued on to Crystal Palace. At one point or other in the second half of the twentieth century, it saw operation by any or all of the garages sited along or near its routeing, namely, Merton, Sutton, Thornton Heath, Croydon, Elmers End and even the short-lived Carshalton. When DMSs replaced RTs in 1973 it belonged mostly to Merton, and allocations fluctuated repeatedly in the next decade and a half until concentration at Sutton in 1988 as part of the Suttonbus network. That was when its last forays beyond Morden to Crystal Palace were withdrawn. Thereafter, vehicle rotation was straightforward, with Ms replacing the DMSs in 1991 and NVs replacing the Ms in 1998. In 2001 Connex Bus was awarded control and held on for fifteen years, through the renamings to Travel London (2007) and Abellio (2009). TA-class Tridents gave way after their expected lifespan to Volvo B7TLs, but in 2016 Arriva London South won the 157 and put refurbished Enviro400s onto it, based at Thornton Heath but with Norwood drivers.

LEFT: The smart new bus station at West Croydon is the location of Thornton Heath's T 127 (LJ10 HVG) on 27 August 2017. This Enviro400 had already been in place for the 109 and 198 since 2010.

BELOW: T 147 (LJ60 AVU) was a later transfer south from Tottenham, where its career had begun on the 341. On 31 May 2020 it is at the top of the steep hill at Crystal Palace.

New in 1981 as a means of clipping off the top end of the overly-long 58, the 158 began with Walthamstow DMSs and had converted by the end of the year to Titan operation. This was still the case when London Forest, the LBL subsidiary created in this part of town, went on strike after the workforce refused to accept the conditions offered in order to retain operation of the 158 and other routes upon their tendering in 1991. The routes were re-awarded and Capital Citybus stepped up with second-hand Metrobuses in yellow, variously from Northumberland Park or new premises taken at Hackney. New Dennis Tridents (TNLs) freshened up the route in 2001 but the next contract, in 2005, was awarded to Stagecoach, which introduced Tridents of its own, based at Stratford until reallocation to Bow in 2006. In 2008 it was transferred to Leyton and in 2011 passed to West Ham. In 2019 Arriva London North won the contract and put it into Edmonton with Volvo B9TLs (VLWs) acquired earlier from Tower Transit and often bolstered by indigenous HVs.

RIGHT: On 17 April 2021 Edmonton's HV 203 (LK66 HCH) is coming into Stratford bus station, with a DW leaving in the opposite direction.

BELOW: The usual complement on the 158 is a batch of ten ex-Tower Transit Volvo B9TLs renumbered into the old VLW class; here at Chingford Mount on 10 May 2019 is VLW 903 (BN61 MXM), new as VN 37965.

159

Marble Arch, Oxford Circus, Piccadilly Circus, Trafalgar Square, Westminster Bridge, Kennington, Brixton, Streatham Hill, Streatham Station.

ABELLIO (QB) – Wrightbus New Routemaster (LT)

Forever famous for fielding London's last regular Routemasters on 9 December 2005, the 159 has long been a an extremely intensive north-south trunk service, once linking Camden and Croydon before its north end was redirected to West Hampstead and its southern end pulled successively back to Streatham. The 159 has variously been operated by any or all of Camberwell, Brixton, Streatham, Thornton Heath and Croydon garages over the years, but the desire to remove multiple-garage operation in the run-up to privatisation concentrated it at Brixton (part of South London) by 1994, at which point a band of RMs received red and cream livery. Its central London leg had had the West Hampstead run taken away in 1992 and Marble Arch was now the terminus. For its last decade as a crew route, RMs and RMLs were mixed in operation and in 1998 were repainted red with only the cantrails taking Arriva's secondary stone colour. A late rally saw daily crew operation restored in 2002 and this led up to the epic finale in 2005. VLAs replaced the Routemasters and these were joined by DWs in 2011, spanning a short-lived extension to Paddington Basin (2007–10). Abellio won the route in 2015 and introduced Borismasters from its Battersea garage.

LEFT: Coming round Piccadilly Circus on 13 September 2020 is LT 624 (LTZ 1624).

BELOW: After being taken back from South Croydon, the southern terminus of the 159 was Streatham garage. Its forecourt remained long after closure, but eventually a new stand was constructed and on 31 May 2020 LT 640 (LTZ 1640) is almost there.

160

Catford, Sangley Road, Middle Park, Eltham, New Eltham, Edgebury, Chislehurst, Queen Mary's Hospital, Sidcup Station.

ARRIVA LONDON NORTH (DT) – Alexander Dennis E40D (T)

Historically a Catford–Welling link since 1938 and with some roads to itself, the 160 was never what you would call hard pressed, even with occasional dives off route into burgeoning estates, and its requirement only breached double figures when Catford replaced its RTs with SMSs in 1970. In 1978 DMSs took over and Ts followed in 1983, but in 1985 the administrative problem of there being a Sunday 160A that proceeded on to Bexley Hospital was solved by introducing the 160 on Sundays and pushing it on from Welling to Bexleyheath. It remained second-tier and was thus demoted to LSs in 1987 and to SR minibus in 1989, at which point it lost the Eltham–Bexleyheath leg to new route B16. Even redeploying the full-size Dennis Lances (LAs) in 1994 couldn't raise its status, but in 1996 something finally worked: the decision to remove the fussy circular 228 and 328 pair linking Eltham and Sidcup and append their routeing to the 160. New DAL-class Darts into Catford now had solid work to do and were often supplemented by Titans and Volvo Olympians. TAS-class Tridents came in 2002 but in 2007 Catford's grip was broken with the 160's award to Arriva Kent Thameside. Dartford has since retained it, replacing the initial transferred DLAs (2006) with Enviro400s (2011–present).

RIGHT: T 316 (LK65 ENF), one of the newer batch of Enviro400s at Dartford, is setting off from Sidcup on 23 August 2020.

BELOW: New to Dartford for the 160 and known for its first four years as Arriva Kent Thameside 6468, Dartford's T 298 (KX61 LDO) is coming into Eltham on 17 April 2021.

161

North Greenwich Station, West Parkside, Charlton, Woolwich, Queen Elizabeth Hospital, Eltham, Mottingham, Chislehurst (War Memorial).

STAGECOACH SELKENT (PD) – Alexander Dennis E40H

Always linking Woolwich and Chislehurst but then famously never quite sure which way to proceed thereafter, the 161 has variously headed south to Petts Wood, east to Sidcup and even west to Bromley before being curtailed at Chislehurst for good in 1994. Historically Sidcup garage's responsibility, with on-and-off participation from Plumstead and/or Abbey Wood as fit, the route operated RTs until 1977 and RMs after that, though Abbey Wood fielded crew MDs until its closure in 1981 and then handed them to the new Plumstead. Both garages received Ts in 1982, followed by OPO conversion in 1985, and in the last two years of Sidcup's own existence help came from Ms and then Ls. After 1988 Plumstead took sole charge and itself converted to Ls. Its Sidcup leg having withered away, the 161 was projected to Bromley North in 1991 and reallocated to Bromley to give that garage work it desperately needed, but in 1994 its award to Kentish Bus with new Volvo Olympians fixed it as Woolwich–Chislehurst once again. Kentish Bus struggled here and was obliged to ditch the 161 in 1995, but Metrobus stepped up and held it for the next twenty years, first with Olympians, then Tridents (2001) and Scanias (2006). In 1999 it had been extended far beyond Woolwich to North Greenwich, and this remained the northern terminus when Stagecoach won it in 2018, introducing new E40Hs from Plumstead garage.

LEFT: Back at Plumstead for the first time since 1994, the 161 now uses E40Hs like 12438 (SN67 XEC), seen at Woolwich on 3 November 2019.

BELOW: At the Eltham station mid-point of the 161 on 17 April 2021 is Plumstead's 12442 (SN67 XEG).

162

Beckenham Junction, Park Langley, Bromley, Bickley, Chislehurst, Imperial Way, New Eltham, Avery Hill, Eltham Station.

METROBUS (MB) – Alexander Dennis E20D

Introduced in 1994 as a permanent solution to the long-standing question of what to do with the 161 once it reached Chislehurst, the new 162 inherited its third possible direction towards Bromley and then combined that with the 126's former Bromley–Beckenham Junction section. Kentish Bus Darts were in charge and in fact this route was the only one to survive the otherwise quick crumbling of that company's over-ambitious Lewisham-area network, principally through reallocation from Lewisham to Dunton Green garage in 1996. Even so, it became a pawn in some unilateral swapping of distantly-operated routes between Arriva (as subsequently incorporated Kentish Bus) and Stagecoach in 1997, which took it to Bromley. Fortuitously, only double-deckers were available, firstly Titans and later its own batch of Volvo Olympians, but in 2001 the 162 received its own batch of Dart SLFs to accompany a re-routing to Eltham via roads that could only accommodate the shortest chassis available. In 2006 Arriva Kent Thameside, heirs to Kentish Bus, won it back with red Dart SLFs out of Dartford, but in 2011 Metrobus secured the tender and added its own Dart SLFs; with that company's retention of the route in 2016 E20Ds, again of the shortest possible length, have come onto the 162.

RIGHT: On 28 February 2021 8.8m E20D 184 (YX62 DZU) serves Bromley South.

BELOW: 175 (YX61 ENT) is at Eltham on 17 April 2021; this wasn't the original routeing of the 162, which had started by turning south to Petts Wood once it had reached Chislehurst.

163

Morden Station, Hillcross Avenue, Lower Morden, Grand Drive, Raynes Park, Wimbledon Chase, Hartfield Road, Wimbledon Station.

LONDON GENERAL (AL) – Alexander Dennis Enviro200 (SEN, SOE) and E20D (SE)

Created in 1987 to clip off the Wimbledon–Morden end of the 156, the 163 continues to link those points by the roundabout route via Raynes Park and Lower Morden. New with surplus LSs put into Merton, it was double-decked in 1988 with DMSs and reallocated to Sutton as part of Suttonbus, but in 1990 some of that network's output was outstationed to Colliers Wood. A year after that, Merton absorbed Colliers Wood's runout, and at the same time the DMSs gave way to Ms. In the privatised era under London General, the 163 was retained by London General in 1996, on the basis of conversion to LDP-class Dart SLF single-deckers. A second generation of these followed in 2001, and in 2009 came SOEs, with a smattering of new E20Ds added alongside in 2015.

LEFT: Its all-over red repaint gleaming after refurbishment against a second contract, Merton's SOE 29 (LX09 AZR) serves Wimbledon station on 30 September 2017.

BELOW: Merton's E20D SE 281 (YX65 RRZ) is setting off from Morden station on 2 September 2018, about to swing round the one-way system here and head for Lower Morden.

Only half the route it used to be, the 164 once continued on beyond the London border to hang a ninety-degree turn west and proceed on beyond Banstead to Epsom. Always Sutton garage's responsibility, it progressed from STLs to utility Daimlers (Ds) and then to RTs, which it kept until 1976. The Routemasters it took on at that point, however, lasted only three years as one-manning with DMSs was implemented in 1979. Although everything south of Belmont was stripped away in 1982 when Surrey County Council refused to subsidise cross-border links any more than it felt was necessary, the 164 expanded from Morden instead, being extended to Lower Morden in 1983 and to Wimbledon in 1984. The latter projection didn't take on the first attempt but was achieved permanently in 1988. Metrobuses replaced the DMSs as part of general fleet upgrading in 1992, but the 164 fell into London General's purview upon privatisation and was defended vigorously when its turn for tender came up in 1996. This involved restocking with new Dart SLF single-deckers, and since then a second generation of LDPs (2001) and two of its successor Enviro200s (2009 and 2016) have operated it. In recent years Merton have taken over responsibility for operation, with Sutton only on Sundays.

**RIGHT: SEN 37 (YX61 FZW)
was new as First DMV 44278,
coming with Blue Triangle's
acquisition of the 368 and
subsequently passing to
Merton. It is in the middle of
the Sutton one-way system
on 5 April 2018.**

**BELOW: SOE 22 (LX09 AZF) with
Optare Esteem bodywork is
coming up to Wimbledon on
23 June 2018.**

165

Romford (The Brewery), Romford Market, Gidea Park, Hornchurch, Abbs Cross Lane, Elm Park, South Hornchurch, Cherry Tree Lane, Rainham (Abbey Wood Lane).

STAGECOACH EAST LONDON (NS) – Alexander Dennis E20D

Circumstance has turned what used to be the major local route in this area, and the last at the old Hornchurch garage to use Routemasters, into a minibus service. Linking Collier Row and Rainham since introduction in 1940, the 165 was Hornchurch's bread and butter and its loss to Ensignbus on tender in 1988 doomed the garage. Until then it had been DMS-operated since 1973 and used Ts since the last days of 1978, but under Ensignbus blue and silver Metrobuses were the staple, amid a vast variety of double-deckers based at Dagenham. In the ensuing quarter-century Ensignbus became Capital Citybus and then First Capital, and the buses were repainted yellow and then red. However, the 165 and its subsequent partner 365 were then repositioned so that the latter became the senior partner, and in 2001 the 165, by now going no further north than Romford, was demoted to DML-class Dart SLFs. The next generation of single-deckers comprised Enviro200s, also known as DMLs, and in 2013 Stagecoach's win of the 165 precipitated First's pulling out of London bus operations. Now based at Rainham, the 165 has seen out one contract with E20Ds and begun another with 18-reg MMC upgrades of the same.

LEFT: Coming into Romford on 5 April 2019, Rainham's 37533 (YX68 UMH) is on its way to the Brewery, a more useful traffic objective than the Market stand used until 2006.

BELOW: 37526 (YX68 UMA) is in Hornchurch on 13 September 2020. The MMC body is fussy in that the black-painted under-bumper sections are rarely restored when panel replacements are undertaken.

166

West Croydon (Bus Station), South Croydon, Purley, Coulsdon, Chipstead Valley, Banstead (Marks & Spencer), Drift Bridge, Epsom, Epsom General Hospital.

ARRIVA LONDON SOUTH (TC) – Alexander Dennis Enviro200 (ENL)

Better known today as a straight run down the Brighton Road to Purley and Chipstead Valley, the 166 between 1970 and 1990 had an eastern arm operating to Shirley and Beckenham Junction. This was when SMS replaced its RTs at Croydon, though DMSs came in 1973. Being lesser in standing than other local routes, it was demoted to LSs in 1987 when a surplus of that single-deck type became pressing, though DMSs soon returned as well as Olympians (Ls) that had since come to Croydon; Metrobuses (1986–87) and Titans (1991–92) were also operated briefly. After being pulled back to Croydon, it was subject to an unusual transfer in 1992 which transferred it on tender from one LBL subsidiary (South London) to another (Selkent) and put into distant Bromley with Titans. This proved inefficient, and in 1997 what had become Stagecoach Selkent swapped it for one of what was now Cowie South London's more local services and back came Croydon, this time with an L and M mix. Single-decking with Darts (LDRs) followed in 1998, at which point a peculiar addition by Epsom Buses was incorporated that took the 166 way beyond Chipstead Valley to Epsom, and this endures. Vehicles since then have been multiple generations of Dart SLFs (DPPs and DDLs), DAF SB120s (DWLs) and E20Ds (ENLs).

RIGHT: On 25 April 2017 Croydon's ENL 26 (LJ58 AVC) is turning into West Croydon bus station, ready for a journey beyond Chipstead Valley to Banstead.

BELOW: Its provenance given away by the orange seat rails, ENL 107 (LX11 AWC), in a revamped Croydon town centre on 30 August 2019, used to be Stagecoach East London 36269.

Always the unique link between Barkingside to Loughton across the London border, the 167 has switched back and forth between single- and double-deckers depending upon which way it turns once out of Loughton station, for there is a low bridge there. From 1950 it was one of the stalwarts of the small but fondly-remembered Loughton garage, initially with STDs and then, between 1955 and 1971, with RTs. OMO came thereafter with SMSs, though in 1976 the upper deck returned when DMSs were put in. Their replacement by Titans at the start of 1982 proved short-lived when the extensive changes of that 4 September imposed LSs, and these ushered out London Transport operation when the garage's entire complement was lost on tender. Eastern National now took over with its own Nationals (which underwent an intermediate company renaming to Thamesway), but struggled and Grey-Green took their place in 1992 with Ikarus-bodied DAFs. New Dennis Dart SLFs were introduced in 1997, but another new operator beckoned in 2002 as Docklands Buses. This firm was taken over by Go-Ahead in 2007 and its MCV-bodied Dart SLFs became part of Blue Triangle's fleet, first from Rainham and then River Road (2016). In 2017 Stagecoach won it and uses E20Ds based at Barking garage.

LEFT: The 167 was briefly one of a number of Barkingside-area routes to have its buses distinguished by discreet branding. Barking's 36662 (SN17 MMF), leaving Loughton station on 9 September 2018, has the requisite blue flashes.

BELOW: Seen in Ilford on 13 September 2020, 36660 (SN17 MMA) is wearing Stagecoach's latest logo.

168

Hampstead Heath, Belsize Park, Chalk Farm, Camden Town, Euston, Holborn, Aldwych, Waterloo, Elephant & Castle, Bricklayers Arms, Old Kent Road (Tesco).

METROLINE (HT) – Wrightbus New Routemaster (LT)

Introduced in 1986 as the sectionalisation of the northern end of the long north-south trunk route 68, the 168 inherited its Chalk Farm share but with OPO Titans working as far south as Elephant & Castle. Tendering saw it pass to Grey-Green in 1990 with new Volvo Citybuses and it would stay there, company name changes and internal reorganisations notwithstanding, for the next quarter-century. Not long after Grey-Green became Arriva London North-East in 1998, operation was transferred from the original garage at Stamford Hill to the nearby London Transport-derived site, and by the time the 168 was moved again to Tottenham in 2000, new DLAs were in service. These gave way to new VLWs later in the decade, and in 2005 the extension down the Old Kent Road to the large Tesco there freed pressure on the stands at the Elephant. The Arriva London North contract of 2010 saw reallocation to Ash Grove and conversion to Enviro400 (T), but in 2015 Metroline broke the streak and put the 168 into Cricklewood with E40H hybrids (TEHs). It was quickly converted to Borismaster (LT) and, while Cricklewood was being rebuilt and enlarged, spent 2017–18 at Holloway. In 2021, however, to accommodate the input of route 328, Cricklewood transferred the 168 to Holloway once again.

RIGHT: Coming round the Elephant & Castle the 'wrong' way from its previous conventional roundabout layout is Holloway's LT 645 (LTZ 1645) on 22 May 2021, just transferred from Cricklewood again but yet to have its garage code changed.

BELOW: LT 657 (LTZ 1657) is entering the useful Waterloo bus station on 22 May 2021.

The 169 has the Ley Street corridor north of Ilford to itself since introduction in 1961, just like its trolleybus predecessor 691. It is at each end that expansion has come; the familiar Clayhall run was added in 1965 and, south of Barking, to Thames View Estate in 1982, although the latter leg was turned over to more local routes in 1987. In terms of buses operated, RTs gave way to DMSs in 1973 and Ts appeared in 1980. Single-deckers made their debut when DAF SB220s (DAs) in silver were transferred by necessity from another route in 1993, with Dart SLFs replacing them in 2001 and double-deckers (Dennis Tridents) returning in 2006 for another contract with the incumbent Stagecoach East London (convened in 1994). For 2011 new Enviro400s were introduced and these have stayed for the next successive contract, with some of them briefly branded at the end of the decade, with green accents.

LEFT: On 26 March 2017 Barking's 19757 (LX11 BDO) is seen heading south through Barkingside.

BELOW: 19783 (LX11 BGU) is coming into Ilford town centre on 18 April 2019.

170

Victoria Station, Royal Hospital Road, Battersea Bridge, Vicarage Crescent, Grant Road, Clapham Junction, Wandsworth, Putney Heath, Roehampton (Danebury Avenue).

LONDON GENERAL (SW) – Alexander Dennis Enviro200 and E20D (SE)

This route's story is one of quick expansion and then slow decline thereafter. New in 1950 to replace tram route 31, it linked Wandsworth and Hackney and in 1959 was extended north-east to Leyton. Withdrawals then followed, however, pulling the 170's extent back to Hackney (1966), Shoreditch (1969), Euston (1971), Aldwych (1982) and Clapham Junction (1991). OMO in 1971 introduced DMSs to replace the RTs, Wandsworth having settled as the southern operating garage and eventually the only one. To accompany the extension at the southern end to Roehampton in 1981, Stockwell took over operation (on Saturdays at first and then altogether in 1982) and in 1984 used the route as a testbed for four trios of experimental buses, though after two years of trials DMSs returned until the route was transformed into a shuttle in 1991. DR-class Darts were now the staple, though over the next decade, as privatised London General replaced London Buses Ltd, the 170 bounced between Stockwell, Merton and Putney garages as capacity permitted, and all had their own kinds of Darts, from DWs to DRLs and DPLs. Stability ensued in 2002 with a contract using LDP-class Dart SLFs allocated to Stockwell, and in 2008 a minor renaissance occurred when the 170 was extended from Clapham Junction to Victoria over the withdrawn 239. London General won it twice more, in 2010 introducing a mix of new Enviro200s (SEs) and transferred long Dart SLFs (DPs), but in 2017 the Wrightbus Streetlites taken for the next contract were found to be too tall for the low bridge at Battersea, so were swapped with 14-reg SEs.

RIGHT: SE 52 (YX60 EOK) was one of the 170's new Enviro200s in 2010 and has remained at Stockwell after refurbishment; on 23 May 2019 it is mid-route at Clapham Junction.

BELOW: On the other side of the tracks at Clapham Junction on 3 December 2020 is SE 205 (YY14 WEC), new to New Cross for the 286 but swapped with a Streetlite.

171

Elephant & Castle, Camberwell, Peckham, New Cross, Brockley Rise, Catford, Catford Garage.

LONDON CENTRAL (NX) – Alexander Dennis E40H (EH)

Once stretching across town from north to south, tram replacement 171 lost its northern section in 1986 to new route 171A (now 341) and the stub into town has withered to the extent that the massive cuts of 2019 pulled it out of central London altogether. To the south, it has been transposed twice and both times with routes called 172; at its start in 1950 it reached Norwood but was altered to terminate at Forest Hill. In 1994 it took over the current 172's roads to Catford garage and continues to turn there. New Cross provided Routemasters until 1986, Titans till 2001, Volvo B7TLs (PVLs) after that and today's fare comprises EHs.

LEFT: Seen turning round at St George's Circus on 12 September 2019 for a journey south is New Cross's EH 175 (YY67 URC). The 171 can now get no further north than this point and passengers from south-east London now have to get two buses.

172

Aldwych, Waterloo, Elephant & Castle, Bricklayers Arms, Old Kent Road, New Cross, Brockley Rise.

LONDON CENTRAL (NX) – Alexander Dennis E40H (EH)

New in 1992 as a renumbering of the self-contained southern section of the 141, the 172 used to reach Catford Garage and either Grove Park or Bromley North until pulled back to Brockley Rise in 1994. Abellio operated the route between 2011 and 2018, but London Central returned and EHs from New Cross are the staple.

LEFT: Brockley Rise may have been the 172's southern terminus since 1994, but less clarity has surrounded where to stand it in central London; it has terminated variously at Liverpool Street, St Paul's, Ludgate Circus and now Aldwych. Heading south from Waterloo on 31 January 2020 is New Cross's EH 173 (YY67 URA).

173

Goodmayes (King George Hospital), Little Heath, Chadwell Heath, Becontree Heath, Dagenham Heathway, Ripple Road, Newham Way, Beckton.

STAGECOACH EAST LONDON (BK) – BYD DD

The innermost section of the once-lengthy 175, route 173 was DMS-operated upon its creation in 1973 and, at that point, linked Poplar with Becontree Heath. Upon its reallocation from Upton Park to Poplar garage in 1978 it was withdrawn between Canning Town and Poplar, and the following year saw it lose its upper deck through comversion to LS operation, which was the price of an extension to Stratford. West Ham took over in 1981 and double-deckers returned in 1984 in the form of Titans, though tendering came early to the 173 and in 1987 Grey-Green took it on with ex-South Yorkshire Fleetlines. It would remain based at this company's Barking garage for the next thirty-three years, though the company itself became part of Arriva. The route was diverted to East Beckton in 1993 and extended at the other end to King George Hospital, at which point single-deck operation returned, first with grey and green Darts and then, from 2000, Dart SLFs in red. 2010's contract saw new Enviro200s introduced, but the next one (2015) specified double-deckers, which were transferred Enviro400s. Finally, Stagecoach won it in 2020 and borrowed Enviro400s from London United to use from Barking until its own batch of electric BYDs entered service at the start of 2021.

RIGHT: Immediately south of Dagenham Heathway on 27 March 2021 is Barking's 14128 (LF70 YVD).

BELOW: Coming up to the 173's East Beckton terminus on 27 March 2021 is 14115 (LF70 YUL). The bus station here was rebuilt on a larger scale on the opposite side of the Asda as its predecessor.

174

Harold Hill (Dagnam Park Square), Hilldene Avenue, Romford, Oldchurch Road, Dagenham Road, Oxlow Lane, Dagenham Heathway, Dagenham (Marsh Way CEME).

STAGECOACH EAST LONDON (RM) – BYD DD

Busy and significant in its local area, the 174 dates from 1950 and assumed its unique run round the eastern edges of Dagenham and Romford to points north shortly after. By the end of the decade North Street had assumed majority operation, Barking only dropping its Saturday share in 1971. RM operation lasted between 1966 and 1982, when Titans appeared, and in 1983 these Ts lost their conductors. By this time the awkward stand at Noak Hill, Pentowan, had been abandoned due to the need for a reversing manoeuvre, but the greater need on Saturdays persisted and between 1986 and 1990 an express service was operated on that day of the week. Stability set in, with the Titans outlasting privatisation of their East London LBL subsidiary under Stagecoach in 1994 and operating until 2001, when TASs (Dennis Tridents) took over. In 2009 the 174 was reallocated from North Street to Rainham to accompany the attempt by the ELBG, holding company between 2006 and 2010, to set up a low-cost unit, and in 2010 Enviro400s were introduced. In 2015 the 174's top end was re-routed to Harold Hill in replacement of withdrawn route 374, and the fulfilment of Stagecoach's contract applying from 2020 has just seen the route's conversion to new BYD electric double-deckers.

LEFT: Brand new electric 14112 (LF70 YUH) is seen at Romford on 27 March 2021.

BELOW: Captured between Dagenham Heathway and Dagenham proper on 13 February 2021, Rainham's 14140 (LF70 YVS) has picked up a coating of road dust.

175

North Romford (Hillrise Estate), Collier Row, Romford, Queen's Hospital, Roneo Corner, Becontree Heath, Dagenham Heathway, Dagenham (New Road).

ARRIVA LONDON NORTH (DX) – Wrightbus Gemini 2 (DW)

Once a tremendously long route linking the East End with rural Essex, the 175 contracted to its current form in 1973, settling with Upton Park garage. After a short period of former BEA Routemaster operation in 1975, RT operation resumed but RMs came for good in 1977, though OMO was inevitable here and Titans were put in place in 1982, losing their conductors the following year. All forays beyond the GLC border had come to an end by then and the southern terminus depended upon Ford Motor Company's presence at Dagenham; when that finished in 2017, New Road became the full-time terminus. North Street's Titans lasted nearly twenty years on the 174, being replaced by Dennis Tridents only in 2001. In 2017 a new operator for the route beckoned in the form of Arriva London North, whose Barking garage used refurbished Gemini 2s of middle years.

RIGHT: The conversion of the 38 to Borismaster operation released large numbers of DWs for use as bidding tools by Arriva, and most of that batch now reside at Barking, for the 175, and Grays for the 103 and 370. South of Romford on 17 September 2019 is DW 255 (LJ59 GVE).

BELOW: On 27 March 2021 Barking's DW 247 (LJ59 AAN) has just passed Dagenham Heathway station.

176

Tottenham Court Road Station, Charing Cross Road, Trafalgar Square, Waterloo, Elephant & Castle, Camberwell, East Dulwich, Dulwich, Forest Hill, Sydenham, Penge.

LONDON CENTRAL (Q) – Volvo B5LH (WHV) and Wrightbus New Routemaster (LT)

New in 1951 as a tram replacement, the 176 gained its characteristic cross-London pattern five years later, at which point Willesden garage joined Walworth. Both shared the route for the next two decades, famously seeing out the last RTLs in 1968 and then featuring the last RTs to work regularly in central London, but Willesden pulled out in 1978 and Camberwell replaced Walworth in 1985, by which time the 176 had been one-manned with Titans. In 1987 it was cut off from Willesden through re-routing within town to Oxford Circus, though a year later it was projected from Forest Hill to Penge to allow some of the 12's Routemasters to be withdrawn. In 1990 it was lost on tender to London & Country, which was obliged to start with tired second-hand Daimler Fleetlines before phasing in new Volvo Citybuses in two-tone green. This operation was moved within its holding group to Londonlinks in 1995 and the later Cowie organisation reallocated the 176 again in 1997, putting it into Norwood as a red bus route. Ex-Kentish Bus Olympians soon replaced the Citybuses and gained Arriva repaints to underscore just the latest ownership. In 2004 new Volvo B7TLs (VLAs) took over and ran until 2016, when London Central's tendering victory introduced Volvo B5LHs from Camberwell. Lately, with reductions to the 12, a proportion of Borismasters (LTs) has been specified alongside the WHVs.

LEFT: Camberwell's LT 417 (LTZ 1417) at Elephant & Castle on 12 September 2019 exemplifies the recent partial allocation of Borismasters. Since 2008 the 176 has reached no further into town than Tottenham Court Road.

BELOW: Crossing Waterloo Bridge on 27 March 2021 is Volvo B5LH WHV 177 (LF67 EXL).

For many years running straight down the Old Kent Road into south-east London, the 177 replaced tram routes 36 and 38 in 1952 and spent the next three decades shared between New Cross and Abbey Wood garages. RTs gave way to DMS OMO in 1972 and when Abbey Wood closed (briefly having fielded MDs), Plumstead took over as the minority garage. Titans reached Plumstead in 1982 and New Cross at the end of 1983, and for a while a 177 Express operated with specially-liveried Titans. In 1988 New Cross came off and Plumstead, now operating Ls, continued alone. The service past Elephant & Castle to Waterloo dwindled and disappeared, and in 1994 the central London ambition was erased entirely when the 177 was diverted at New Cross to Peckham. It was thus ripe for single-decking, taking Darts in 1996 and being diverted off the main roads through the Abbey Estate, but this proved too much and double-deck operation returned in 1999 with Volvo Olympians. Low-floor buses came in 2003 in the form of Dennis Tridents and the next two Selkent contracts used Scanias (purchased in 2008 when the ELBG group was in charge of Selkent) and Volvo B5LHs (in 2015, with Stagecoach in charge again).

RIGHT: The Wright-bodied Volvo B5LHs into Plumstead in 2014 were got rid of quickly, but the Enviro400 MMC-bodied followup batch for the 177 has stayed put. Here at Greenwich station on 2 May 2021 is 13078 (BJ15 TWC).

BELOW: On 28 February 2021 Plumstead's 13076 (BJ15 TWA) is passing through Woolwich.

178

Woolwich, Queen Elizabeth Hospital, Shooters Hill Road, Kidbrooke Park Road, Kidbrooke Station, Ryan Close, Lee Green, Lewisham.

LONDON CENTRAL (MG) – Alexander Dennis E40D (E)

New in 1980 to localise the Woolwich–Abbey Wood end of the 180 and push it further on into Thamesmead, the 178 broke out of its box through an extension in 1981 to Lewisham via Kidbrooke, taking that role over from the former 291. This was when Plumstead MDs replaced Abbey Wood DMSs, but in 1983 Titans took over and three years later Olympians supplanted the Ts in turn. 1988 saw the 178 become part of the notorious Bexleybus network, being reallocated to a reopened Bexleyheath and treated to elderly DMSs and leased Olympians. This lasted only three years, but the winning of the network by London Central, another LBL subsidiary at the time, ensured stability. Titans were now in charge, but in 1994 the closure of the road bridge at Kidbrooke station obliged curtailment of the route there and conversion to DRL-class Darts. These spanned the privatisation of London Central that year and continued until 1999, when Stagecoach Selkent won it and put it back into Plumstead with SLD-class Dart SLFs. Restored through to Lewisham in 2004, the 178 was reallocated to Catford in 2006 and its Dart SLF complement refreshed; between 2013 and 2016 its path through Kidbrooke changed as the Ferrier Estate was demolished and replaced by Kidbrooke Village. Upon its takeover by London Central in 2018, it was double-decked with Es, anticipating Elizabeth Line traffic which hasn't yet happened. New Cross was in charge at first, with Morden Wharf taking over in 2019.

LEFT: After seven years at New Cross, WVL 275 (LX59 CYO) spent time at River Road and Merton garages before coming to Morden Wharf, in whose hands it is seen at Woolwich on 6 February 2021 in lieu of an E.

BELOW: E 260 (YX12 FPV) was also an original New Cross motor, but on 6 February 2021 is seen at Woolwich.

179

Ilford (Hainault Street), Gants Hill, South Woodford Station, Woodford Green, Woodford Wells, Whitehall Road, Chingford Station.

STAGECOACH EAST LONDON (T) – Alexander Dennis E40D

With most of its corridor to itself, the 179 dates from 1963 when it was hived off from the 145 and given the Thames View Estate end of the 193. Barking garage had responsibility, with RTs until 1969 and OMO SMSs thereafter; DMSs restored the upper deck in 1974 and Titans took over Barking's routes in 1980. The Barking–Thames View section was removed in 1982, and in 1985 an unusual method of ensuring that a neighbouring garage could stay in business saw it reallocated to Loughton and extended there from Chingford. Loughton could only field LSs so the 179 got them, and when this garage inevitably closed in 1986 the route passed to Leyton, still under LSs. Tendering saw the 179 lost to Grey-Green in 1987 and Leyland Lynxes took over. In 1996 Capital Citybus won the route and converted it back to double-deck using Dennis Arrows in a yellow livery. By the next victorious bid for this route, the company had become First and in 2001 gave it Dennis Tridents (TNs). Enviro400s (DNs) followed after that, seeing the route's cutting back to Ilford in 2010, but in 2013 Stagecoach East London won the 179 and took new E40Ds of its own. These were intended to be replaced by new buses in 2018, but in the event stayed put, though the route was reallocated to Barking, bringing it full circle.

RIGHT: 10179 (SN63 JWF) has an Edinburgh registration booked by the Falkirk arm of Alexander Dennis's bodying capacity, and on 24 September 2017 is seen at Gants Hill.

BELOW: Now carrying a blind with wider-spaced route number characters, Barking's 10174 (SN63 JWZ) has arrived at Ilford on 13 September 2020.

180

Lewisham, Greenwich, Charlton, Woolwich, Plumstead, McLeod Road, Abbey Wood, Yarnton Way, Crabtree Manorway, Belvedere Industrial Area.

LONDON CENTRAL (MG) – Volvo B9TL (WVL)

The main carrier between Woolwich and Lewisham over the main drag, the 180 was historically shared between Abbey Wood and Catford until the former closed in 1981 and the new Plumstead took majority responsibility. Crew-operated MDs replaced its RMs and in turn gave way to Titans before one-manning in 1983, and Plumstead re-equipped in 1986 with Ls. Over time its routeing south of Lewisham was removed, though a diversion to Hither Green proved abortive. In 1998 new operator Harris Bus took over, with blue and green Volvo Olympians based at a site at Belvedere (conveniently right at the 180's eastern end), but this company crumbled quickly and was reconstituted in 2000 as East Thames Buses, with red repaints for all. New Volvo B7TLs introduced in 2002 satisfied the low-floor imperative and these VWLs lasted until 2017, when Belvedere was allocated refurbished Volvo B9TLs (WVLs). Belvedere's closure in that same year saw operation transferred to the new garage at Morden Wharf near Greenwich.

LEFT: New to Peckham for the 63, WVL 323 (LX59 DCF) was refurbished after that route's conversion to MHV operation and sent to Belvedere for the 180. Now based at Morden Wharf, it is seen at Greenwich on 3 June 2018.

BELOW: On 30 June 2019 WVL 330 (LX59 DDE) is coming past new construction at Woolwich, where the new Elizabeth Line station will eventually open.

181

Lewisham, Hither Green, Sangley Road, Catford, Bell Green, Lower Sydenham, Southend Lane, Downham, Grove Park Station.

STAGECOACH SELKENT (KB) – Alexander Dennis E20D

New in 1984, the 181 was given the task of combining the less valuable Lower Sydenham end of the 180 with hitherto-unserved roads in the Hither Green area. It was allocated to Catford with LSs, and a year later was extended from Lewisham over the withdrawn P5 to Surrey Docks. Re-routing in 1987 took the 181 to Lower Sydenham from the west instead of the east and added a further extension to Rotherhithe, but its roads north of Lewisham passed to new route 225 in 1989, the same year as SR minibuses were introduced. In 1994 it was awarded to Kentish Bus and converted to Dennis Dart operation, but the new operator struggled from the outset and in 1996 was obliged to give the 181 up, at which point Metrobus took over with its own Darts. In 2001 Catford returned, now under Stagecoach Selkent, this contract specifying Dart SLFs. Since then it has been back and forth with Metrobus, which won the 181 back in 2006 and introduced new Scania N94UDs to accompany an extension to Grove Park. In 2018 Stagecoach Selkent were victorious again, but this time operation was from a new base at Kangley Bridge Road. The type operated is now Alexander Dennis E20Ds.

RIGHT: Making its way round the awkward new road layout at Lewisham on 17 April 2021 is Kangley Bridge Road's 36686 (SN67 XBO).

BELOW: Passing through Catford on 23 August 2020 is 36694 (SN67 XBX).

182

Harrow Weald (Oxhey Lane), Wealdstone, Harrow, Northwick Park Hospital, Sudbury, Wembley Central, Neasden, Staples Corner, Brent Cross Shopping Centre.

METROLINE (HD) – Volvo B5LH (VWH)

So long that it had to be split into three sections, the 18 gave its middle section to new Harrow Weald and Alperton MB-operated route 182 in 1970, though the Watford Junction leg tacked on at that time didn't last long. Alperton soon took full charge and the Merlins gave way to DMSs in 1974, with Metrobuses taking over in 1980. The route sidestepped the Harrow Buses programme of 1987 but in 1990 was put into Harrow Weald to save that garage from closure when everything else had been lost. In 1999 its long-serving Ms were replaced by Dennis Tridents (TAs), though the last Metrobuses at Harrow Weald didn't all leave until 2004. In 2004 Harrow Weald replaced its Tridents with Volvo B7TLs (VPs) and these ran until 2016, when a new contract accruing to Metroline saw new Volvo B5LH hybrids (VWHs) phased in.

LEFT: Crossing the mouth of Harrow bus station on 20 July 2020 is Harrow Weald's VWH 2201 (LK16 DHE).

BELOW: Since 1999 the northern end of the 182 has been at Oxhey Lane, a little further north than Harrow Weald garage, in which it used to turn. VWH 2210 (LK66 DXC) is a little further south still when seen amid a break in the clouds on 23 December 2019.

183

Pinner (Love Lane), North Harrow, Harrow, Kenton, Kingsbury, West Hendon, Hendon, Golders Green Station.

SOVEREIGN (BT) – SCANIA N230UD (SP) and Volvo B5LH (VHR)

Long the conduit out of Golders Green to points west, the 183 was the reason for Hendon garage's existence through years of RTs (1954), DMSs (1975) and Ms (1980). After Hendon's closure, Harrow Weald took it on and later in 1987 incorporated a shortened route into the troubled Harrow Buses network with a type change to leased Mark II Metrobuses and second-hand Volvo Ailsas. The 183 came out of this still based at Harrow Weald and with proper Ms returning; its LBL subsidiary Metroline was privatised in 1994 and blue skirts appeared on the buses. In 1999 tendering saw the route awarded to Sovereign and new blue and cream Dart SLFs took over, but the single-deckers were hard pressed and in 2001 new Volvo B7TLs in red and black were introduced. Sovereign have held on ever since, despite ownership of the company bouncing between two French state undertakings. In 2009 new Scanias took over and have been the staple ever since, with six Wrightbus SRM-bodied Volvo B5LHs bolstering the allocation since 2017, all from Edgware garage. The latest contract will see conversion to electric operation with the delivery of a quantity of BYD DD double-deckers.

RIGHT: Familiar on the New Routemaster, Wrightbus's SRM body enjoys a different profile on Volvo B5LHs. Only eight were built and Sovereign had six; this is VHR 45208 (LJ66 EZU) at Harrow on 18 September 2019.

BELOW: On 2 September 2018 all-Polish Scania N230UD SP 40073 (YT59 RXX) turns at Pinner, the terminus of the 183 since 1987.

184

Turnpike Lane Station, Wood Green, Durnsford Road, Bounds Green, Arnos Grove, Hampden Square, New Barnet, Barnet Church, Barnet (Chesterfield Road).

LONDON GENERAL (NP) – BYD D8UR (SEe)

Today's 184 has known two other identities in its role as busy outer-suburban link, first as 261 and then, from 1982, as 84A. The current number was imposed in 1996 over the existing Dennis Dart (DRL) operation from Wood Green garage, by then part of Cowie Leaside, and over the years just the vehicle complement changed according to contract terms, with DAF SB120s (DWLs) being introduced in 2002 and Alexander Dennis Enviro200s (ENLs) in 2009. One double-decker was also operated at school times. A rather fussy mode of operation in 2014 kept the buses at Wood Green but staffed them with drivers based at Edmonton, but this proved short-lived. In 2021 the 184 was tendered again and this time won by London General on the basis of electric single-deck operation, comprising new SEe-class BYDs operated out of Northumberland Park garage.

LEFT: On 20 February 2021 Northumberland Park's new SEe 124 (LF70 YWB) has just come to the end of a route 184 journey to Turnpike Lane.

BELOW: SEe 143 (LF70 YWX), seen at Wood Green on 20 February 2021, is the highest-numbered of the batch allocated to Northumberland Park for the 184, though SEes already based for the 153 and 214 can also now visit.

Victoria to Lewisham the long way round, the 185 used to continue on to the southern head of the Blackwall Tunnel until the 1980s. It was mostly Walworth's responsibility, with Catford added in 1972 and then Camberwell replacing Walworth in 1985, but tendering catapulted the route into notoriety. London Easylink's takeover in 2001 saw new Volvo B7TLs (VPs) replace the long-established Titans, but the newcomer's ignominious collapse in 2002 forced a host of emergency operators to put out anything they could for some months until a combination of London Coaches (Arriva's tours brand) and East Thames Buses could restore stability. The latter was given the contract on a long-term basis in 2003 and restored the VPs. These continued on when East Thames Buses was bought by Go-Ahead in 2009, now working from Camberwell, and in 2014 spare VLWs (Volvo B7TLs) replaced them. The London Central contract applying from 2016 specifies new buses, these being a mix of E40Hs (EHs) and Volvo B5LHs (MHVs), though WHVs from the 188 are also common.

RIGHT: Visiting from the 188 on 3 June 2018, Camberwell's WHV 184 (LF67 EXT) is passing new architecture at Victoria.

BELOW: MCV EvoSeti-bodied Volvo B5LH MHV 71 (BV66 VGE) is at Lewisham on 14 December 2018. Substantial reconstruction is also evident here, completely altering the road layout in this busy town centre.

186

Northwick Park Hospital, Harrow, Wealdstone, Canons Park, Edgware, Mill Hill Broadway, Grahame Park, Hendon Central, Brent Cross Shopping Centre.

METROLINE (HD) – Volvo B5LH (VW)

New in 1970 to replace the outermost section of the 18, route 186 began with SMSs from Edgware, though Ms replaced them in 1980. Hendon garage participated with its own Ms between 1985 and closure in 1987, and in 1991 the route passed under a LBL (Metroline) contract to Harrow Weald, where it has remained, although Metroline was privatised in 1994. In this year the route was chosen to host the first production low-floor buses, the LLW class of Dennis Lances, and these endured until 2006, with the last two years of that span seeing them operated from Edgware. Double-deckers returned in the form of VPL-class Volvo B7TLs and in 2007 Alexander Dennis Enviro400s (TEs) took over. A significant intermediate re-routing in 2010 took the 113 off the Watford Way dual carriageway and pushed it through Grahame Park instead, and the final change so far has been a reallocation from Edgware back to Harrow Weald in 2018 and conversion from TE to VW operation.

LEFT: VW-class Volvo B7TLs were a rarity at Harrow Weald but grew in number with the input of the 186. Seen leaving Brent Cross on a rainy 24 November 2019 is VW 1287 (LK12 AOX).

BELOW: Metroline has always juggled fussy mixed allocations of buses, depending on what's newest; VW 1283 (LK12 AOA) is coming into Harrow on a sunny 20 July 2020.

187

Central Middlesex Hospital, Harlesden, Kensal Rise, Queens Park, Warwick Avenue, St. John's Wood, Swiss Cottage, Finchley Road (Sainsbury's).

METROLINE WEST (WJ) – Alexander Dennis Enviro200 (DE)

Introduced in 1940, the 187 soon took its classic South Harrow to Hampstead Heath configuration and then dwindled. Generally shared between Alperton and Middle Row until the latter's closure in 1981, the route was converted from RM to M in 1982 and cut back to West Kilburn. Single-decking followed in 1990, with Darts (DRs) based at North Wembley under a Metroline (LBL) contract, but in 1999 London Traveller took over with Volvo B6BLEs, at which point the route was curtailed at Central Middlesex Hospital from the east so that new route 487 could assume the western end. An extension to the east in 2000 brought the 187 back as far as Finchley Road. London Traveller was renamed Metropolitan Omnibus in 2000 and passed under Thorpes' ownership at the end of 2002, and the 187's award to First in 2004 saw Dart SLFs (DMs) take over, operated by Willesden Junction garage. Such has been the case ever since, though DMLs (Alexander Dennis Enviro200s) replaced the DMs in 2009 and these became DEs upon First's sale of its operations in this sector to Metroline.

RIGHT: Substantially rebuilt in recent years, Central Middlesex Hospital plays host to Willesden Junction's DE 1650 (YX09 AEA) on 5 January 2019. This bus was new as First DML 44083.

BELOW: DE 1636 (YX58 FOH), delivered as First DML 44060, is at Harlesden on a gloomy 10 December 2019.

188

Russell Square, Holborn, Aldwych, Waterloo, Elephant & Castle, Bricklayers Arms, Rotherhithe, Canada Water, Surrey Quays, Deptford, Greenwich, North Greenwich.

LONDON CENTRAL (Q) – Volvo B5LH (WHV)

Now settled as a link between central London and Greenwich, the 188 underwent an extraordinary variety of operators in the early tendering era, hopping from Boro'Line Maidstone (1989) to LBL (1990), London & Country (1993), Londonlinks (1995), South London (1997), Arriva London North-East (1998) and Arriva London North (2000) before a more stable period beckoned at the end of that year with its award to London Central (though even here, it was London General which actually assumed operation). Its wild spell had actually been carried out with the same Volvo Citybuses, with just the operators changing hands or positions within their corporate group, but under London General's Stockwell it fielded Volvo B7TLs (PVLs). Between 2002 and 2004 Camberwell also had an allocation. In 2005 Travel London won the 188 and introduced new Wright-bodied Volvo B7TLs (Vs), this company becoming Abellio in 2009. Hybrid Alexander Dennis E40Hs followed a little after the contract applying from 2010, but after five years plus two added for good performance, the 188 was lost to London Central with new Volvo B5LHs (WHVs) from Morden Wharf. These were reallocated to Camberwell in 2018 with the route's operation and remain there.

LEFT: On 17 September 2019 Camberwell's WHV 186 (LF67 EXV) is seen at Waterloo.

BELOW: Its smooth running choked off in recent years by anti-terrorist barriers and now cycle lanes, Waterloo Bridge is the location for this 27 March 2021 shot of WHV 182 (LF67 EXR).

189	Marble Arch, Baker Street, Lisson Grove, Abbey Road, Kilburn, Cricklewood, North Cricklewood, Brent Cross Shopping Centre.
	METROLINE (W) – Wrightbus New Routemaster (LT)

New in 1997 to replace route 16A, the 189 continued its function of linking Brent Cross with the West End, though via Abbey Road and Lisson Grove rather than straight up the Edgware Road. It began with DLD-class Dart SLFs based at Metroline's Cricklewood and although the operating company and garage have remained the same, the vehicle complement has changed; Dennis Tridents (TPs) ran between 2003 and 2010, followed by a consignment of Enviro400s (TEs). The TEs gave way to hybrid TEHs in 2012, with a new batch of these coming in 2013, and in 2016 the 189 was selected for conversion to Borismaster (LT). Structurally, there has been some wavering over where the route should stand in central London, and in 2017 it was withdrawn between Marble Arch and Oxford Circus so that the 113 could be restored to the latter terminus.

RIGHT: On 18 July 2017 Cricklewood's LT 794 (LTZ 1794) is rounding Marble Arch at the end of a typical route 189 journey.

BELOW: About to turn off Baker Street to serve a diversion on 21 March 2021 is LT 652 (LTZ 1652), allocated to Cricklewood earlier for the 168, but now able to work on the 16 and 189 as well.

190

West Brompton (Empress State Building), Lillie Road, Hammersmith, Stamford Brook, Chiswick Bridge, Richmond (Bus Station).

METROLINE (AH) – Alexander Dennis Enviro200 (DM)

The most recently introduced member of the '90' family of routes, the 190 was new in 1991 to take over the Hammersmith–Richmond end of the 290 and carrying on to West Brompton. It operated Leyland Lynxes from Stamford Brook (LBL), later converting to Darts, but a quirk of tendering at this point handed London Buslines a Sunday service on the 90, which lasted until 1996. That was when Armchair took over, with orange and white Darts based at Brentford, and the same set-up exists today, though long since taken over by Metroline. In 2002 red and black Dart SLFs were taken for the route, and in 2009 came the current MCV-bodied Enviro200s.

LEFT: Metroline took a liking to MCV's sales pitch in the second half of the 21st century's first decade, ordering its body on both MAN 12.240s and Alexander Dennis Enviro200s. One of the latter is Brentford's DM 963 (LK09 EKL), seen pulling into Richmond bus station on 20 April 2019.

191

Brimsdown Station, Carterhatch, Forty Hill, Chase Side, Enfield Town, Ponders End, Alma Road, Nightingale Road, Edmonton Green Station.

ARRIVA LONDON NORTH (DW) – Wrightbus Gemini 2 (DW)

New in 1954 to hack round some Enfield-area backstreets, the 191 was substantially reoriented in 1982, losing its service across the Lea Valley Reservoir to Chingford in favour of replacing the old 135 to Brimsdown. Enfield started it under London Transport and now have it again under Arriva, though in 1996 it was taken over by Thamesway, which gave way to First Capital in 1998 and to London General in 2013.

LEFT: Arriva London North's standard fare in the declining days of diesel double-deckers is the Wrightbus Gemini 2 Integral. One allocated to Enfield is DW 575 (LJ13 CJF), seen in Enfield Town on 3 November 2020.

192

Enfield Town, Bush Hill Park, Bury Street, Edmonton Green, Montagu Road, Angel Road (Tesco), Watermead Way, Tottenham Hale Station.

ARRIVA LONDON NORTH (E) – Alexander Dennis E20D (ENN)

Actually the second route of this number to be operated by Enfield, today's 192 began in 1995 with StarRider minibuses pointed through some tricky backstreets within sight of Edmonton Green and away from the usual approaches to Enfield from this direction. Bigger buses were phased in over the year, first 8.5m Darts (DTs) in 1996 and then 9m examples (DRNs) in 1998 before the low-floor imperative brought 8.8m Dart SLFs (PDLs) to accompany another Arriva London North contract in 2002. The extension to Tottenham Hale via the warehouse-outlet district in Angel Road caused the route's popularity to explode, and by then it was fielding twice as many buses as it had when new. Arriva's further award of the 192 in 2007 was accompanied by the delivery of new Enviro200s (ENs) and a reallocation to Lea Valley garage, though it was restored to Enfield in 2013. The following year saw London General awarded the 192, and Northumberland Park took over with new Wrightbus Streetlite WFs (WSs). However, Arriva won it back in 2019 and this contract's fare consists of new Alexander Dennis E20Ds, coded ENN.

RIGHT: On 3 November 2020 Enfield's ENN 71 (YX69 NYU) begins the turn into the revamped one-way system at Enfield Town.

BELOW: On the final leg of a journey to Enfield Town on the afternoon of 24 April 2021 is ENN 65 (YX69 NYN).

193

Romford (Queen's Hospital), Romford Market, Romford Station, Osborne Road, Hornchurch, Suttons Lane, Hacton Lane, Wingletye Lane, County Park Estate.

STAGECOACH EAST LONDON (NS) – Alexander Dennis E20D

Today's 193 bears almost no resemblance to the direct replacement for trolleybus route 693 introduced in 1959. Then linking Hornchurch and Barking 'round the corner' via Ilford, the route was completely restructured upon its one-manning in 1982, now operating no further west than Romford. This set it up for tendering and its concurrent loss to Eastern National in 1985, but that operator, latterly known in that sector as Thamesway and subsequently falling under First Capital, managed to keep hold of it for the next twenty-eight years. During this era it was converted to minibus in 1986 and expanded out of its Hornchurch box through a re-routing to County Park Estate over the former 256. The buses themselves comprised Mercedes-Benz 608Ds, followed by two separate generations of 709Ds and eventually Optare Solos, but in 2013 First closed down and Blue Triangle took over the 193, inheriting former First Dart SLFs which it reclassified DMNs. In 2018 Stagecoach won the route and put it into North Street with new E20Ds.

LEFT: On 5 December 2018 North Street's 37521 (YY18 TKN) exemplifies Stagecoach East London's current offering at Romford station.

BELOW: 37521 (YY18 TKN) is seen again, this time on 27 March 2021, coming round the complicated one-way system surrounding Romford.

194

Lower Sydenham (Sainsbury's), Sydenham, Penge, Beckenham, Elmers End, West Wickham, Shirley Way, East Croydon, West Croydon (Bus Station).

ARRIVA LONDON SOUTH (TC) – Wrightbus Gemini 2 (DW)

An old route with many decades of history in the Croydon, Shirley, West Wickham and Beckenham areas, the 194 has in more modern times been pulled back successively from its furthest ambitions, ceding its Forest Hill terminus in 2003, whilst the forays south of Croydon to Purley Way (the old Croydon Airport) were transferred to the 119 in 1996. There were also various examples of 194A, 194B and 194C, though only the 194B was substantial enough to last the distance and is today known as 198. The 194 was historically the bread and butter of Elmers End garage, which closed in 1986; Croydon took over, but in 1992 a tendering result took it off what had by then become the South London subsidiary of London Buses Ltd and gave it to Selkent, which operated it from Bromley with Ts replacing its long-established DMSs. Volvo Olympians (VAs and VNs) appeared in 1998 and low-floor Tridents (TASs) in 2000, but Arriva London South won the contract in 2003 and back came Croydon, this time with DWs (DAF DB250LFs). This firm's retention of the route two more times saw the complement freshened in the second instance in 2019, refurbished Gemini 2s (also known as DWs) being transferred from Tottenham to Croydon.

RIGHT: DW 305 (LJ10 CVN) came to Croydon when the 149 was converted to Borismaster in 2015, and on 12 January 2019 is seen at West Croydon bus station.

BELOW: Another transfer from elsewhere is DW 263 (LJ59 LXU), new to Clapton for the 38 but displaced from there by a Borismaster in 2014. It is at East Croydon on 27 August 2017.

195

Charville Lane Estate, Church Road, Hayes & Harlington Station, North Hyde Road, Southall, Ealing Hospital, Hanwell, Boston Manor, Brentford (County Court).

ABELLIO (GW) – Alexander Dennis E20D

The second route 195 to pick its way round the Hayes area, this incarnation was introduced in 1971 as a Hanwell SMS operation. Metrobuses replaced these at the end of 1979 and in 1985 Hanwell took over. In 1986, the route passed to London Buslines with yellow ex-DMSs, but this independent kept it for only one term before London Buses Ltd won it back in 1991 and put it back into Hanwell, this time with MA-class Mercedes-Benz 811D minibuses. Hanwell closed in 1993 and the new Greenford premises operated the 195 thereafter; its holding company, Centrewest, was privatised in 1994 and in 1996 was sold to First, whose financial backing produced a large number of new DM-class Dart SLFs. These lasted from 1997 until 2003, but this time newcomer Ealing Community Transport won it, using new Caetano-bodied Dart SLFs. In 2008 the route was extended from Ealing Hospital to Brentford. As it turned out, ECT pulled out in 2009 and First returned, soon phasing in new Enviro200s (DMLs). During the period of Hayes garage operation (2010–15), First sold its assets in this sector to Metroline in 2013. In 2015 the 195 was restored to Greenford, but Metroline West lost the route to Abellio when tendering came again in 2017. Since then E20Ds have been the staple, based first at Teddington premises and switching to Hayes and back before permanent reallocation to the new Southall garage in 2019.

LEFT: Southall's E20D 8885 (SN17 MPU) is at Southall Broadway on 24 April 2021.

BELOW: On 1 April 2019 8881 (SN17 MOV) is at Hayes & Harlington Station.

196

Elephant & Castle, Kennington Lane, Vauxhall, Lansdowne Way, Stockwell, Brixton, Herne Hill, Tulse Hill, West Norwood, Norwood Junction.

ABELLIO (QB) – Alexander Dennis E40H

New in 1950 as an Archway–Waterloo link, the 196 soon expanded southwards to Norwood Junction, but in 1974 was curtailed from the south at Brixton, turning it into a local route that nonetheless remained busy. OPO came in 1982 with Camberwell Titans, though a switch to Norwood in 1985 saw it converted to Ms. Ex-South Yorkshire Fleetlines became the fare during the unhappy tenure of Cityrama (1986–89) but new Volvo Citybuses (VCs) formed the basis of London General operation from 1990, after it bedded in at Stockwell with DMSs. Even so, it was first in the line for reallocation elsewhere if staff shortages pressed, with the result that Camberwell had it back for a spell (1997–99) and even distant Metrobus participated. In 2001 it was won by Connex and allocated new Tridents (TAs) from Beddington Cross; five years later, following a useful extension to Elephant & Castle, London General's Stockwell took it back with the first of its E class of Enviro400s. This contract was renewed in 2011, but in 2018 Abellio (successor to Connex) regained it, this time using E40Ds and operating them out of Walworth garage.

RIGHT: Walworth's 2589 (YY67 GZK) was ordered against the 45, but in this 8 December 2020 shot at Vauxhall is seen on the 196.

BELOW: One of the 196's proper batch of E40Ds, 2618 (SN18 KLL), is seen on the new southbound west side of the former Elephant & Castle gyratory on 4 August 2018.

197

Croydon (Fairfield Halls), East Croydon, Cherry Orchard Road, Norwood Junction, Anerley, Penge, Sydenham, Forest Hill, Dulwich, Peckham Rye, Peckham.

METROBUS (C) – Alexander Dennis E40H (EH)

Long established as a simple link between Norwood Junction and Croydon via Woodside Green, the 197 has expanded beyond either terminus and fallen back, only to break out again. Its most famous leg beyond Croydon to Caterham was sectioned off upon transfer from London Buses Ltd's Croydon garage to London Country in 1986, and didn't return despite Croydon taking back the route in 1990 and hanging on to it until 2019. Instead, the 197 found itself projected northwards to Peckham over the 312 in 2005, bringing some significance back to the route. In Croydon's time since resuming responsibility, it had fielded Ms, followed by Ls and then DLAs and DWs. Metrobus's contingent, operated out of its own Croydon premises, comprise E40Hs.

LEFT: One slightly annoying change imposed upon the 197's switch of operators was to pull the 197 back from its Katharine Street terminus at Croydon to Fairfield Halls, severing an important link. Not that there is anyone around to visit the latter on 6 February 2021, whether by EH 341 (YW19 VVO) or any other means.

BELOW: EH 341 (YW19 VVO) is seen again, this time at Penge on 21 March 2021.

198

Thornton Heath (High Street), Thornton Heath Pond, West Croydon, East Croydon, Shirley, Shrublands.

ARRIVA LONDON SOUTH (TH) – Alexander Dennis Enviro400 (T)

New in 1992 as a straight renumbering of the 194B in order to get rid of its suffix, the 198 began with Bromley Titans, but in 1997 the impracticality of such distant operation was recognised by Stagecoach Selkent, which swapped it with South London for a more local route. Thornton Heath thus took over and have remained in charge ever since, though the Ls used then gave way to DLAs in 2003 and Ts (Enviro400s) in 2010.

RIGHT: New to Palmers Green for the 102 and subsequently sluiced south, Thornton Heath's T 5 (205 CLT, ex-LJ08 CVW), seen at West Croydon on 23 August 2020, carried this former Routemaster registration for over a decade.

199

Catford Garage, Catford, Lewisham, Greenwich, Deptford, Pepys Estate, Surrey Quays, Canada Water Station.

STAGECOACH SELKENT (TL) – Alexander Dennis E40D

There have been three 199s in the last half-century, all anchored on the Bromley Road and all as a means of taking work off part of the 1. This latest one hails from 1991, at the time linking Elephant & Castle and Catford Garage with Catford Titans. This garage has remained in charge, though coming under Stagecoach Selkent in 1994 and replacing the Ts with Volvo Olympians, then Dennis Tridents and two kinds of Enviro400. In connection with the Jubilee Line extension in 1999, the 199 fell back from the Elephant to Canada Water.

RIGHT: On 18 April 2019 Catford's 11001 (YY18 TKZ) is coming through Lewisham town centre.

200

Raynes Park, Copse Hill (Atkinson Close), The Ridgway, Wimbledon, Queens Road, Haydons Road, Merton, Colliers Wood, Phipps Bridge Estate, Mitcham (Fair Green).

LONDON GENERAL (AL) – Volvo B5LH (WHV)

Long a fixture in the nicest parts of Wimbledon, the 200 has always had ambitions eastward, reaching Mitcham via Phipps Bridge and then variously serving Wallington or even Streatham Hill. The latter terminus was in use when years of Merton operation, first RFs, then DMSs, gave way in 1986 to a miserable two years with newcomer Cityrama. This firm struggled to cope with its blue DMSs until surrendering the contract voluntarily, at which point Kingston Bus stepped in on a temporary basis using LSs from Norbiton. A longer-term gig was awarded to LBL's London General in 1989, using Ms from Colliers Wood, an ultimately short-lived outstation of Merton, which took on the route in full in 1991. Four years later the route was split across Mitcham as 200 and 201 and converted to DPL-class Dennis Dart operation, and single-deckers endured when Mitcham Belle won both in 2000, these being Dart SLFs in red, white and blue. Mitcham Belle faltered and its collapse in 2004 gave rise to Contra, which managed to be even worse, but in 2006 Merton came back to the 200 under London General, soon phasing in Enviro200s (SEs) which lasted until 2020 when spare Es double-decked the route again, followed by spare WHVs. The current contract is awaiting new electric Optare Metrodeckers.

LEFT: Normally domiciled on the 280 at Merton, WHV 29 (LJ61 NVR) is seen on the 200 on 9 May 2021, passing through the new road layout at Mitcham.

BELOW: Filling in until the 200's electrics come is WHV 80 (BF65 WKE), new to Metrobus at Croydon but made spare with the loss of the 202. It is seen at Raynes Park on 9 May 2021.